**PUBLISHING DIRECTOR** Sarah Lavelle
**COMMISSIONING EDITOR** Stacey Cleworth
**SENIOR DESIGNER** Gemma Hayden
**PHOTOGRAPHER** Issy Croker
**ILLUSTRATOR** Evi-O.Studio | Emi Chiba
**HEAD OF PRODUCTION** Stephen Lang
**SENIOR PRODUCTION CONTROLLERS** Katie Jarvis, Lisa Fiske

Published in 2022 by Quadrille,
an imprint of Hardie Grant Publishing

Quadrille
52–54 Southwark Street
London SE1 1UN
quadrille.com

Text © Meg Abbott 2022
Photography © Issy Croker 2022
Illustration © Evi-O.Studio | Emi Chiba
Design and layout © Quadrille 2022

Cataloguing in Publication Data: a catalogue record for this book
is available from the British Library.

Every effort has been made to ensure the information in this book is
up to date. However, availability of facilities and opening hours are,
of course, subject to change. Furthermore the publishers and authors
can accept no liability for any injury, loss, illness or accident sustained
by anyone as a result of following advice or information contained in
this book.

978 1 78713 846 9

Printed in China

# THE LAKE DISTRICT

## Where to Eat, Sleep and Explore

MEG ABBOTT & ISSY CROKER

*Hardie Grant*

QUADRILLE

# CONTENTS

# INTRODUCTION

Misty peaks and glassy waters, plunging valleys, ancient paths and wide open skies; bustling pubs, snoozy villages and market towns in the shadows of mountains. The land of the Lake Poets, Alfred Wainwright's 'silent forests' and Beatrix Potter's traditional farms is a UNESCO World Heritage Site. Every inch of its ancient tracks and soaring peaks is protected and nurtured, giving the whole place the feeling of a precious artifact, unspoilt by the outside world. You don't so much visit the Lake District as disappear into it.

England's biggest National Park is a place that's been inspiring writers and artists for centuries. Many spent their entire life nobly trying to put its magnificence into lines of poems or strokes on a canvas. Wordsworth is probably the most celebrated Romantic of the lot; he dedicated most of his life to putting the beauty of this mystical place into words, urging us all to leave city life behind and throw ourselves into nature. As I sit on a rock, drying off beside the shore of Coniston Water, the famous lines 'And then my heart with pleasure fills, And dances with the daffodils' drift into my mind. When you're here immersed in nature, it turns out that Wordsworth makes perfect sense.

We talk a lot these days about 'unplugging'; from technology, from tiresome routines, from everyday life. And while it's true you don't have much choice in the Lake District (or 'The Lakes'), where phone signal is often non-existent, it's the place itself that has this effect. When nature is this enticing and soothing, you want to be fully present for it. The air is clean and sweet with Scots pine, the pace is slow and thoughtful, and the landscape is so utterly, beautifully daunting it forces you to be mindful of

every step. Instead of scrolling on your phone you'll be gazing at the thumbprint of the moon reflected in the tarns at night, at the clouds' shadows racing across the fells and at the sun spilling through the gently swaying forest canopies. The Lake District is a place of light and sound, drama and absolute peace. Dwarfed by mountains the colour of bruises, this idyllic place leaves you feeling inspired, refreshed and completely calm.

A trip here scratches the travel itch. It's a place that beckons you outside, filling your days with activities and adventure. This is England, but not as we know it. From certain angles, it could be the Alps, soaring mountains set against trembling fields of flowers; from others, it could be the mountains of upstate New York or the open roads of the midwest. Thick forests of fern and almost tropical-looking flora conjure the New Zealand rainforest and there were a few times, winding through thick forests with the sun beaming through sky-high trees, we said in unison 'Canada?'. And yet, there is a quintessential Englishness that pervades every corner of this place. Hotels range from the deliciously luxurious to the wonderfully unique, with plenty of cheerful B&Bs that you'll never want to leave. No walk is complete without a boot-sized slab of something sweet, served with a dollop of cream and a pot of restorative tea. Pubs serve tepid, flat Cumbrian ale (the proper stuff) to chattering walkers. Proud gardeners tend to their rose gardens in the foot of the fells. Whisper-quiet cafés serve hot buttered crumpets and cups of milky tea, while fellwalkers are fed by glistening full English breakfasts. And no one would dream of passing you by on a quiet street without a friendly (but restrained) 'Hello!'.

# LAKE DISTRICT
## National Park

N
W    E
S

Bassenthwaite Lake

Skiddaw

KESWICK

Blencathra

PENRITH

Loweswater

Crummock
Water

Derwentwater

Ullswater

Thirlmere

Haweswater

Ennerdale Water

Buttermere

Helvellyn

Wastwater

GRASMERE

High Street

ESKDALE

Scafell Pike

AMBLESIDE

HAWKSHEAD

Lake
Windermere

WINDERMERE

The Old Man
of Coniston

CONISTON

KENDAL

Black Combe

Coniston
Water

CARTMEL

## SOME FAVOURITES:

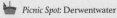

Picnic Spot: Derwentwater

View Point: Cat Bells

Rainy Day Activity: Brunswick Yard

Cycle Hire: Lowther Castle and Gardens

Pub: The Drunken Duck

Gift Shop: Perfect English

Wild Swimming: Kailpot Crag

Sunbathing Spot: Rydal Water

# GETTING AROUND

There's no bad way to explore the Lake District. All it asks of you is to be out in it, craning your neck at the peaks of the fells, slipping into its cool waters, stomping up hills and losing your way in sun-dappled forests. The landscape is England's most dramatic, soaring and jaw-dropping. This place brings out the explorer in everyone, whether you are a seasoned hiker or someone who prefers to take in the views from the window of a car en route to your next pub lunch.

We drove around the Lakes. If you do have a car (or want to rent one), this is probably the best way to see the area and gives you the ultimate freedom to explore. Parking is easy, and most popular walking routes have easy-to-find car parks at the starting line. You usually have to pay, but you'll rarely struggle to find a space. But not everyone drives, and you can get around just fine if you don't. Good bus services run across the Lake District, with bus stops in most villages and towns. Consider staying in one of the bigger towns like Keswick or Ambleside so you have access to more bus routes, and look out for bus tours if you have a specific area in mind (*englishlakestours.com* is a good place to start). As for getting in and out of the Lakes, Windermere, Staveley, Oxenholme and Kendal all have train stations.

You could return here year after year and barely scratch the surface of the landscape. Our trips are usually around a week long, giving us time to cover more ground and stay in a few different areas. If you're planning a weekend trip, it's best to pick just one or two areas to explore – experience has taught us that trying to fit too much in means you see less of the good bits and more of the main roads.

The Lake District gets pretty busy in the summer. Book ahead if you want to stay in the more popular hotels, and always reserve your table for the evening – there are a few all-star restaurants here that can get booked up weeks in advance. Planning ahead is useful. But if you are anything like us, you will find yourself waking up each morning with a rough itinerary of walks, swims and greedy lunches for the day, allowing plenty of room for altered plans along the way (like when we were ten minutes into a hillside walk and spied a beautiful little tearoom – needless to say the walk was abandoned in favour of whipped cream and fresh cherry pie).

*Left to right: Kirkstone Pass, Coniston Water*

# ABOUT US

We are Meg Abbott and Issy Croker, a writer and photographer duo who just so happen to have been best friends for 17 years. Issy has photographed food and travel for magazines like *House & Garden, National Geographic Food* and *The Sunday Times*. She's also shot cookbooks for the likes of Anna Jones, Gizzi Erskine and Jordan Bourke. Meg writes for brands – everything from art and fashion to tech. And occasionally (when the world is being very kind to us), our love of travel and each other overlaps.

We are the first to admit our obsession with travel is out of control. Downright greedy, in fact. We're always on the hunt for the next fix – that one unforgettable meal, heady night, moment in nature or run-in with a wonderful stranger. We tend to choose the places furthest away, the more hours on a plane or sleepless nights of jet lag conducive to the biggest adventures. Over the years we've travelled side by side, writing stories on markets in Morocco, coffee in Sweden, wine in Tuscany, pitmasters in Texas, street food in Tokyo, foraging in Finland and hiking trails in New Zealand (that last one ended with a mildly serious bicycle accident and a sprained ankle – it was worth it for the view). But lying on a cool shore in the Lake District with no idea of the time, feet half submerged in cold, clean lake water, the sound of it musical and meditative, we came to realise that those moments can be found in the UK, too.

This is our first book together, celebrating the Lake District. We hope in this series we can share what we've learnt recently; that you don't always have to travel somewhere adventurous to find adventure.

# ABOUT THIS BOOK

This book is by no means a complete guide. There's so much more for us to see, and we plan to. Rather, think of this as a snapshot of the off the beaten track Lake District as we see it, where mountains are there to be climbed, paths to be cycled, tarns to be swum, forests to get lost in. We're celebrating this magical region by producing a thoughtfully curated guide with the best places to eat, sleep and explore. We hope this inspires you to dive into the Lakes.

## HOW TO USE THIS GUIDEBOOK

Travellers do not make their way through the world alphabetically, and neither does this book. In the upfront section of the guide, there are recommended routes as well as feature pages highlighting some of our favourite things to do. The main chapters are ordered by area and you'll find our recommendations within each – these are by no means a comprehensive list, but a considered and thoughtful selection of our favourite places. Happily, walking and wild swimming are free, and open to all. We've given detail and directions in the book and you should be able to find your way independently (the Lakes are well signposted, but do carry a detailed map for longer walks). As for other activities like boating, watersports and group swimming, it's best to ask locally about availability and price (there are often options for shorter rentals in case you want to keep the costs down).

Within the local areas it's easy to get between each place in very little time. Please note that the chapters do not all follow exactly the same pattern – the destination dictates what is and isn't included.

## RESERVATIONS

The Lake District is a popular destination and we recommend making reservations in advance for all the places to eat and sleep that we have listed in the guide (particularly vital if you are visiting in the school holidays).

## PRICES

It's possible to visit the Lake District on a shoestring, but there are plenty of options if you're looking to treat yourself to something more extravagant. Meals at many of the cafés and restaurants we've included can be enjoyed for around £10–£20 per person, while the delis and farm shops are great options if you want to fill up your backpack before a walk and have an alfresco lunch among the fells. Pubs often offer well-priced two- or three-course menu options.

Accommodation-wise, campsites and Airbnbs are always good low-budget options, and wild camping is allowed if you have permission from the landowner. We've included lots of good mid-budget hotel options (rooms from £100), with a few more high-end places thrown in, too, if you're ready to spend more.

# LAKE DISTRICT ULTIMATE FIRST-TIMER'S PACKING LIST

We'll be honest, the first time we came to the Lake District we packed badly. Terribly, in fact. Within hours, we found ourselves in an outdoor equipment store in Keswick, stocking up on fleeces, thick socks and shoes that didn't let water pour in after five minutes on the fells. The weather can be unpredictable here in the Lakes, so even if the sun is shining when you set off for the day, make sure you pack a couple of layers just in case.

- Lightweight backpack
- Walking shoes
- Thick socks
- Comfy trousers
- Fleece
- Waterproof jacket/coat
- Gloves
- Waterproof hat
- Water bottle
- Flask
- Swimwear
- Lightweight towel
- Map (phone signal isn't always great)
- Picnic blanket
- Penknife (preferably with a corkscrew feature)

# RECOMMENDATIONS

# PICNIC SHOPS

It's not hard to find an ideal picnicking spot in the Lakes. Whether you set off for a sunrise breakfast on a lakeshore, stop for lunch in the shade of an oak tree or have dinner on a peak overlooking the dusky land below, be sure to make use of the myriad local producers in the area. Here is a little selection of our favourite shops for stocking up on picnic essentials (if, like us, you see Cumbrian cheese and wine as essentials).

**CARTMEL VILLAGE SHOP**
Divine sticky toffee pudding and buttery biscuits in Cartmel (see page 142).

**CARTMEL CHEESES AND KESWICK CHEESE DELI**
Specialists in artisan and Cumbrian cheeses.

*1 & 2 Unsworth's Yard, Cartmel, Cumbria, LA11 6PG*
*cartmelcheeses.co.uk | @cartmelcheeses*

*9 Packhorse Court, Keswick, CA12 5JB*
*keswickcheesedeli.co.uk | @keswickcheese*

**RATTLE GHYLL FINE FOOD AND DELI**
Vegetarian delights, artisan snacks and handmade sandwiches.

*Greta House, Rydal Road, Ambleside, LA22 9BS*
*rattleghyll.com | @therattleghyll*

**TEBAY SERVICES FARMSHOP AND KITCHEN**
Fresh pastries, smoked fish and homemade pies (see page 102).

*Left to right: Picnic at Coniston Water, Chesters by the River, Lucia's Coffee + Bakehouse, early evening hike (with our trusty flask) in Little Langdale*

### WINDERMERE WINE STORES AND AMBLESIDE WINE STORE

Expertly-chosen wines with classic French, sparkling and natural varieties to choose from.

*11 Crescent Road, Windermere, LA23 1EA*
*windermerewine.co.uk | @windermerewine*

*6 Compston Road, Ambleside, LA22 9DR*
*lakesdistillery.com/map/ambleside-wine-store*

### LOW SIZERGH BARN

Farm-grown vegetables, ice cream from their own dairy cows and homemade cakes.

*Low Sizergh Barn, Sizergh, Kendal, LA8 8AE*
*lowsizerghbarn.co.uk | @lowsizerghbarn*

### THE HONEYPOT

Busy deli in the heart of Hawkshead selling locally-baked bread, cheese, chutneys and artisan snacks.

*2 The Square, Hawkshead, Ambleside,*
*LA22 0NZ | honeypothawkshead.com*
*@thehoneypothawkshead*

### HAWKSHEAD RELISH COMPANY

Award-winning chutneys and preserves.

*The Square, Hawkshead, Ambleside, LA22 0NZ*
*hawksheadrelish.com | @hawksheadrelish*

### LUCIA'S COFFEE + BAKEHOUSE AND CHESTERS BY THE RIVER

Fresh sourdough, baguettes and pastries (see pages 70 and 114)

### THE CHOPPING BLOCK PENRITH

Cured meats and curated ready-made hampers (see page 82).

# A RAINY DAY

It will come as a surprise to no one that it rains a lot in the Lakes. The weather systems up in the peaks can be totally different from down in the valleys at any given time. You can often find yourself caught in a dramatic rainstorm only for the clouds to part and reveal blistering blue skies moments later – or enjoying a dip in a sunlit tarn only for the skies to blacken as the storm clouds roll in. Rainy weather is pretty much a given on your trip (whatever season you visit), but that doesn't have to be a bad thing. In fact, a drizzly day can paint the place in a rather beautiful light. Think cloud-shrouded peaks, misty fields and crammed pubs with flickering fireplaces. So stay indoors or make like a local, pull on your waterproof and tramp on despite the damp.

It's great to have a rainy day itinerary in mind for those mornings you wake up, throw open the curtains and are met with thick sheets of rain outside. Of course, you could always just grab a good book, head to a pub and cosy up in a corner all day. But here is a rough little itinerary for those who want to carry on exploring despite the wet weather. Another great option is one of the scenic drives (see page 33).

## GRASMERE

**9.00 a.m.** Start with a coffee and fresh-out-the-oven pastry at *Lucia's Coffee + Bakehouse* (see page 70). We recommend their warm, softly spiced cinnamon buns, which you definitely won't want to share. Wander the galleries and bookshops here (*Heaton Cooper Studio*, see page 75, and *Sam Read Bookseller*, see page 75, are great options). Grab an umbrella and join the queue for *The Grasmere Gingerbread Shop* (see page 75).

*Drive 45 minutes northeast via A591 and A66 towards Penrith*

## PENRITH AND AROUND

**10.30 a.m.** Visit *Brunswick Yard* (see page 84), home to more than 20 independent specialist vintage sellers and independent retailers. Pick up a bottle of natural wine from Sam at *Black Hand Wine* and a snack from *The Kitchen in the Yard*.

**12.00 p.m.** Head for lunch at *George and Dragon* (11 mins via A6, see page 82) where the menu changes monthly and most of the produce is grown at their gardens at nearby *Askham Hall*. If you can't get a table here, try their sister pub *The Queen's Head* (7 minutes via A591 and A66, see page 149).

*Drive 1 hour via M6 towards Cartmel (via Tebay Services)*

*Left to right: The Drunken Duck Inn, exploring in the rain*

## CARTMEL

**2 p.m.** On your drive to Cartmel, be sure to stop for artisan snacks, fresh bakes and smoked fish at *Tebay Services* on M6 (southbound). In Cartmel, don't miss a sticky toffee pudding at *The Cavendish Arms* (see page 140), or pick one up to take home from the original creators at *Cartmel Village Shop* (see page 142). Wander around the village for vintage shops, tea rooms, delis and B&Bs.

*Drive 35 minutes north via A592 towards Windermere*

## WINDERMERE AND AROUND

**3 p.m.** Take the ferry across Lake Windermere and drive to the *Beatrix Potter Gallery* in Hawkshead (45 minutes via Windermere Ferry), an exhibition of original illustrations on view in a 17th-century house (*nationaltrust.org.uk*). Catch a late afternoon screening at the *Royalty Cinema* (see page 94).

**7 p.m.** Settle in for a long dinner at *The Drunken Duck Inn and Restaurant* (8 minutes via B6286, see page 110), or for something a little more casual, head to *Base Pizza* in Windermere (97 Lake Road, Bowness-on-Windermere, LA23 3BJ; *basepizzaplace.co.uk*; @basepizza) for delicious wood-fired sourdough pizzas.

# GREAT PUB WALKS

There are fewer pleasures greater than settling into a creaky pub armchair for your first sip of cold beer, your legs buzzing pleasantly from a long day's walking. A trip to the Lake District might come hand-in-hand with exploring the great outdoors, but you can't truly understand the place without exploring its pubs. They are part of the soul of the place, offering comfort and sustenance when you crave it most.

And there are a lot of them. From low-ceilinged inns to pubs where the ale comes with a side of mountain views, you can't go too wrong with the pubs of the Lake District. While some are prettier or more historic than others, all promise the same thing – a snug place to sit, comfort food, free-flowing ale and locals who are part of the furniture.

Follow these well-trodden walks, each as unique and beautifully dramatic as the last, and end in the best possible way – at the pub. Your legs will thank you.

## GREAT LANGDALE AND THE OLD DUNGEON GHYLL HOTEL

Tucked in the pristine Langdale Valley west of Ambleside, *The Old Dungeon Ghyll* (see page 113) has been feeding and watering the Lake District's best climbers for hundreds of years. This walk actually begins at the pub, but you can loop back around and duck in for a few ales once you've finished. Starting in the car park, follow the stony path all the way along the Mickleden Valley – you'll be able to spot climbers up on the grey crags to your right. After a while the valley will open up, revealing wild, rocky wilderness. You'll know it's time to turn around when you spot the dry stone sheep pen. Follow the same route back to the pub.

*Walk time: Around 2 hours*
*Starting point: Old Dungeon Ghyll Hotel car park*

## LOWESWATER LOOP AND THE KIRKSTILE INN

From the car park between Mockerkin and Loweswater Hall, which you'll find between Loweswater and Crummock Water, walk southeast towards Loweswater. Carry on along the road for a few minutes until the lake comes into view to your right. Keep an eye out for a footpath – this will lead you off the road and down onto the beautiful lakeshore. You'll be back on the road soon after that, and carry on walking until you come across the *Kirkstile Inn* (see page 40). After a lunch of traditional pub grub made with the best local produce, re-enter the lakeside walk. It's impossible to go wrong, just keep the water on your right. You'll be able to take in the tranquil water, dramatic

*Left to right: Kirkstile Inn, Tweedies*

views of Grasmoor and Mellbreak, through wide forest tracks and sun-dappled shores all the way back to where you started. Maybe even with a swim thrown in.

*Walk time: Around 2 hours*
*Starting point: The car park between Mockerkin and Loweswater Hall, CA13 0RU*

### WHITBARROW NATURE RESERVE AND MASONS ARMS

Set on a hillside looking out across the Winster Valley in the southern Lakes area, the *Masons Arms* is a 16th-century coaching inn – and a bit of a Lake District institution. To work up an appetite for their hearty, seasonal dishes, start at the pub and walk towards the *Whitbarrow Nature Reserve*. There, you'll find ancient woodland, miles of wildflowers, rare breeds of cattle and carboniferous limestone (laid down around 350 million years ago, no less). Head back to the *Masons Arms* when a craving for ale and lamb rump strikes.

*Walk time: Around 2 hours*
*Starting point: The Masons Arms*
*masonsarmsstrawberrybank.co.uk*
*@masonsarmsstrawberrybank*

### THE TROUTBECK ROUND AND THE MORTAL MAN

You could happily spend a whole afternoon meandering around the lovely village of Troutbeck, which you'll find along the hilly road from Windermere to Penrith. Start this walk at *The Mortal Man* (see page 113), then head south through the village and turn right onto Robin Lane. When you reach Hundreds Road, look out for signs for Wansfell and Nanny Lane just before a stone bridge. This will lead you uphill where you'll get some lovely views of Froswick peaks (among others). Return via Nanny Lane to go back down into Troutbeck (and back to the pub).

*Walk time: Around 1½ hours*
*Starting point: The Mortal Man*

## EASEDALE TARN AND TWEEDIES BAR

Start this lovely hike in Grasmere Village, walking through wind-whipped farmland towards stony, cascading Easedale Beck. After that, you'll reach Easedale Tarn, perched in the upper Easedale Valley with Slapestone Edge and Tarn Crag overlooking its glassy waters. Turn around here and head back to Grasmere. *Tweedies* (see page 69) is the perfect place to end up.

*Walk time: Around 1½ hours*
*Starting point: Grasmere Village*

## SALE FELL AND THE PHEASANT INN

Sale Fell is one of the smaller peaks in the Lake District (perfect for a pre-lunch stroll, if you ask us). It features surprisingly impressive views of the giant peak of Skiddaw mountain, and the views of Bassenthwaite from the summit are mighty. Starting at the layby beside *The Pheasant Inn* (Bassenthwaite Lake, Cockermouth, CA13 9YE; *inncollectiongroup.com/pheasant-inn*), head up the road past Routenbeck. Taking a left, you will join a footpath into the woods. Keep going along the peaceful forest tracks before heading south and joining another footpath to the left. This is where you'll move up the summit and be met with sudden views of Skiddaw. When you've taken it all in, follow the path down and pass through the woods back to the one-time coaching inn, where you can choose from delicate, beautifully-presented seasonal dishes like seafood linguine, Thai red curry or homemade burgers in bouncy brioche buns.

*Walk time: Around 2½ hours*
*Starting point: The Pheasant Inn*

## HELVELLYN AND THE KING'S HEAD PUB

This is a tougher walk. Which means you'll be even hungrier at the end of it. Take the popular route up the giant slopes of Helvellyn, beginning (and ending) at Swirls car park in Thirlmere. It's a pretty straightforward climb to the top – but be warned that the climb goes on for 1½ miles (2.5km). Once you hit Browncove Crags, you'll climb over Helvellyn Lower Man to reach the summit and its mighty panoramic views. Once you've taken in the views (and got your breath back), you can pass over Dollywagon Pike before walking down to Dunmail Raise. It all ends nicely with a forest walk above Thirlmere, before leading you back to *The King's Head* (see page 42), a former 17th-century coaching inn just off the main road where you began. The seat by the roaring fire is the best in the house.

*Walk time: Around 5 hours*
*Starting point: Swirls car park on the A591*

Grasmere

*Blea Tarn*

# WILD SWIMMING

It would be downright wrong to come to the Lake District and not swim. Even for those who don't usually take the plunge, the sight of sparkling tarns and deep, quiet lakes is pretty irresistible. In the summer, the waters of the 16 mighty lakes and hundreds of tarns turn a deep, dark blue, flanked by soaring mountains and oak-studded hills. They're so inviting you may even find yourself parking up on some unmarked roadside and diving in, half-clothed. Of course, anyone with any sense (not us, then) takes swimming gear with them on every walk to prepare for this eventuality.

Here is a handy list of the swimming spots in this guide:

*Derwentwater* (see page 48)

*Black Moss Pot, Langstrath Beck* (see page 48)

*Buttermere* (see page 48)

*Crummock Water* (see page 51)

*Tongue Pot, Eskdale* (see page 62)

*Greendale Falls* (see page 63)

*Rydal Water* (see page 76)

*Stock Ghyll Force* (see page 118)

*Elterwater* (see page 122)

*Loughrigg Tarn* (see page 122)

*Blea Tarn* (see page 124)

*Low Peel Near, Coniston Water* (see page 132)

*Angle Tarn* (see page 153)

*Kailpot Crag* (see page 154)

*Glencoyne Bay* (see page 154)

## TOP TIPS

Do your research online and ask locals about the latest before heading to any swimming spots.

Avoid mooring areas, marinas and jetties – ideally, choose one of the quieter lakes that do not allow boats.

Swim along the shoreline so you can get out easily if you need to.

Only swim when weather conditions are suitable.

Check if the lake or tarn is suitable for swimming. Some places such as Ennerdale Water, Haweswater reservoir, Thirlmere reservoir and Kentmere reservoir do not allow swimmers.

Consider booking a guided wild swim or coached session, like Adventures with Emma (*adventureswithemma.com*; @adventureswithemmalakedistrict) or Swim The Lakes (*swimthelakes.co.uk*; @swimthelakes).

## WILD SWIMMING SAFETY

Take care in deep water – and be very careful on slippery rocks, particularly treacherous on a wet day. Inexperienced swimmers may want to stick to smaller tarns, or just explore the shallow edges of the water. If you are doing more than just dipping, follow the Lake District's SwimSafe Code (*lakedistrict.gov.uk*) and wear a bright swim cap and tow a bright float. Consider wearing a wetsuit if you are going to be in for a while; not only do they protect you from the cold but they also provide buoyancy. In general, tarns (small mountain lakes) are cooler than lakes and can be pretty bracing (even on a hot day). We recommend filling a flask with hot tea and having plenty of layers on hand for when you get out.

# LOCAL BOOKSHOPS

You'll notice a few charming independent bookshops tucked away in the Lake District's towns and villages. Some specialise in local maps and walking routes, while others sell all the Romantic poetry you could need. Here are a handful of our favourites.

## BECKSIDE BOOKS

Two storeys of wonderful antique and second-hand books tucked at the bottom of St Andrew's Churchyard.

*31 St Andrew's View, Penrith, CA11 7YF*

## KERR & SONS BOOKSELLERS

This place has been selling rare books to the people of Cartmel for 85 years, and has over 10,000 books to pore over.

*Priory Barn, Priest Ln, Cartmel, Grange-over-Sands, LA11 6PX*

## THE NEW BOOKSHOP

Browse fiction, non-fiction, children's books and Lake District literature in this friendly, independent bookshop in Cockermouth.

*42–44 Main Street, Cockermouth, CA13 9LQ*

## FRED HOLDSWORTH BOOKSELLER

A favourite with locals and visitors looking for a holiday read, 'Fred's' was opened in 1956. It proudly stocks an eclectic range of books, from international bestsellers to climbing books, geology and maps.

*Central Buildings, Ambleside, LA22 9BS*

## BOOKENDS OF KESWICK

The smaller sibling of the Carlisle branch shop, this bustling bookshop stays busy with visitors buying walking maps and fiction and the odd Wordsworth collection well into the evenings in the summer.

*66 Main Street, Keswick, CA12 5DX*

## SAM READ BOOKSELLER

This award-winning independent bookshop sits at a bustling corner of Grasmere. It's brimming with the best names in the literary world and the Lake District's finest wordsmiths, from Beatrix Potter and John Ruskin to Coleridge and Wordsworth.

*Broadgate House, Grasmere, Ambleside, LA22 9SY*

## HENRY ROBERTS

In this welcoming bookshop on Market Place, you'll find everything from local guides and maps to classic board games and gifts.

*Waverley House, Market Pl, Ambleside, LA22 9BU*

## HEDGEHOG BOOKSHOP

The staff at this independent bookstore are always happy to help if you're looking for something particular (or have no idea what you want at all). Everything is carefully selected and curated to showcase the best new literature and helpful area guides. There's even a little space upstairs to sit and read for a while.

*19 Little Dockray, Penrith, CA11 7H*

# RECOMMENDED ROUTES: SCENIC DRIVES

While walking is all well and good, sometimes you just want to get in the car, make yourself comfy and cover a little more ground. On rainier days (or when your legs are aching from all the fell-climbing), a meandering drive with a flask of something hot can be an adventure. Pack a picnic and something to swim in – you'll most likely end up finding some lovely spots and you wouldn't want to miss the chance to dive in.

For the most part, roads are clearly signed. There are a few drives that require a bit more grit, often heading up into the mountains. Make sure you have a look online if you're planning a particular route, or just stick to the bigger roads to avoid any white-knuckled journeys (especially if you're in a hire car).

## WINDERMERE TO ULLSWATER VIA KIRKSTONE PASS (17 MILES/27KM)

Speaking of 'more grit', this is a great example of a trickier route. It tackles the Kirkstone Pass (the highest mountain pass in the Lake District) – otherwise known as 'The Struggle'. It's a beautiful way to get to the Eastern Lakes, avoiding the busy main roads. Just follow the twisty A592 towards Ullswater from Windermere. You'll have incredible views of Red Screes and Brother's Water along the way, and the sight of Ullswater coming into view is always fantastic.

## CONISTON LOOP (42 MILES/67.5KM)

Make your way through mountains, valleys and villages on this 42-mile loop. Your journey will start in the Langdale Valley, before taking you up over Wrynose Pass and down through beautiful Eskdale. From Eskdale you'll make your way to Duddon Valley, finishing with beautiful views of Coniston Water as you come back into Coniston.

**Left to right:** *Honister Pass, Buttermere*

### KESWICK LOOP
### (18 MILES/29KM)

Starting at Keswick, you'll start by going along the edge of beautiful Bassenthwaite Lake before taking the exit at the *Castle Inn*, where you'll take a country track and pop out on the other side of the lake across the A66. From here, you can loop back to Keswick, with some incredible views of Latrigg and Skiddaw along the way.

### HARDKNOTT PASS
### (13 MILES/21KM)

Connecting Eskdale with the Duddon Valley, the Hardknott Pass currently shares the 'steepest road in England' title with Rosedale Chimney in North Yorkshire. This steep, single-track road is known for being challenging so only drive if you feel confident reversing and handling hairpin bends. The views from the top are exceptional and there is a great pub (*The Boot Inn*) at the top for a drink overlooking the fells.

### BUTTERMERE-HONISTER PASS
### (4½ MILES/7KM)

Honister Pass starts at Gatesgarth Farm, at the southern end of Buttermere. Connecting the Buttermere Valley with the eastern end of Borrowdale Valley, its summit reaches 1167ft (356 metres). Unsurprisingly, it's one of the region's highest passes.

# RECOMMENDED ROUTES: PUBLIC TRANSPORT

The Lake District National Park is working hard to reduce the number of vehicles on the roads, so it is encouraging people to explore other ways of getting around. Consider exploring the region by bus, watch the landscape pass by on a train or get out on the water by boat. Here are some of our favourite options:

## RAVENGLASS AND ESKDALE RAILWAY

This heritage railway allows you to explore some of the area's most inaccessible parts. Once used to transport mined ore from the mines above Boot, the steam train now runs daily services. Hop on board for a journey from Ravenglass to Boot, with lots of pretty stops along the way.

*ravenglass-railway.co.uk*

## THE LAKESIDE AND HAVERTHWAITE RAILWAY

Explore the countryside of the southern lakes with this beautifully preserved railway. Settle down in one of the traditional carriages, pulled by steam locomotives to cover a lot of ground and give your legs a well-deserved break from walking. You can make a day of it with a combined ticket that doubles up as a trip on the Windermere Lake Cruises.

*lakesiderailway.co.uk*

## ULLSWATER STEAMERS

The iconic Ullswater Steamers have been gliding across the lake for over 150 years, ferrying between Pooley Bridge and Glenridding. In fact, one of the steamers is thought to be the oldest working passenger ferry in the world. There are lots of drop-off points around the water, so you can spend the day hopping on and off exploring Ullswater. Book online, or give them a call to secure your ticket ahead of time.

*ullswater-steamers.co.uk*

## KESWICK LAUNCH

While most people go straight to the Ullswater Steamers or Windermere, the Derwentwater Cruises are a brilliant way to explore the dramatic landscape around Derwentwater. These cruises are active all year round, and will take you to some hidden lakeside spots that are inaccessible by car. You can also hire a private boat from Keswick Launch Company, if you fancy a solo excursion.

*keswick-launch.co.uk*

# KESWICK, DERWENTWATER AND NEARBY

# KESWICK, DERWENTWATER AND NEARBY

When exploring the Lakes, Keswick is a good place to start. It is the northernmost hub of the district; a mountain-laced market town with plenty of coffee shops, bakeries and restaurants to fuel your days. The gleaming lakes of Crummock Water and Buttermere lie west of the town centre, so it's the perfect base if you're looking to explore these waters. Keen walkers use the town as a base, setting off early to swim, bike and hike the surrounding landscape, which includes Blencathra and Skiddaw fells. The town is tucked beside Derwentwater, a mighty lake primed for dusky swims and sunrise strolls below the hills.

# EAT

## FELLPACK

After a few too many rounds of pub sausage and mash, this place is a blessing. It specialises in 'Fellpots' – wholesome, all-in-one bowls of goodness like cauliflower carbonara, BBQ pulled jackfruit or mixed bean chilli. Best served with a Lakeside Golden Hour Spritz.

*34 Lake Road, Keswick, CA12 5DQ | fellpack.co.uk*

## THE WAINWRIGHT PUB

This dog-friendly boozer is the perfect antidote to a day out on the fells. Their food is made using largely local produce – all the beef and lamb on the menu come from Cumbrian farms, and the fish is from a local supplier. It's a friendly old place and a favourite with locals looking to be fed and watered. And by 'watered' we mean make use of the many real Cumbrian ales on tap.

*Lake Road, Keswick, CA12 5BZ | thewainwright.pub*

## THE COTTAGE IN THE WOOD

Standing 1,000ft (304 metres) high in the soaring Whinlatter Forest outside Keswick (England's only mountain forest), *The Cottage in the Wood* is a one-Michelin-starred restaurant run by chef Ben Wilkinson. This innovative place is all about celebrating the rich abundance of Cumbria's local produce – the menu changes constantly according to what the seasons have to offer – and has been voted one of the UK's top 25 restaurants (and is consequently booked up months in advance). Take in the stunning views of the forest valley and Skiddaw mountain range from the light-drenched dining room. *The Cottage in the Wood* is also a 'Restaurant with Rooms', with nine tranquil bedrooms upstairs – some with mountain views (minimum stay two nights).

*Magic Hill, Braithwaite, Keswick, CA12 5TW | thecottageinthewood.co.uk
@thecottageinthewoodkeswick*

## KIRKSTILE INN

This classic pub is just the place for some post-hiking refreshment – in our case in the form of a beer paddle with three little glasses from Kirkstile's Cumbrian Legendary Ales brewery. You can't miss the white stone building crawling with roses, right on a crossroads just outside Loweswater. Relax in a velvet booth beneath the dark beams for good beers, friendly bar staff and views over the River Cocker.

*Loweswater, Cockermouth, CA13 0RU | kirkstile.com | @thekirkstileinn*

**Real Ales**
Our current draft Selection

**Loweswater Gold** 4.3%
A pale golden ale made with
mainly lager malt + German hops
producing a tropical fruit aroma +
Flavour. Winner of many awards.

**Langdale** 4%
A Fruity refreshing golden best
bitter with orange marmalade
+ English Fruit Flavour with a long
bitter finish.

**ESTHWAITE** 3.8%
A GOLDEN BITTER WITH THE
DISTINCTIVE FLAVOUR FROM FIVE
DIFFERENT MALTS AND THE
AROMA OF AMERICAN CASCADE
HOPS — CHAMPION BITTER 2013

*Kirkstile Inn*

# SLEEP

## THE KING'S HEAD

Formerly a 17th-century coaching inn, you'll find this popular pub and inn at the foot of Helvellyn Mountain, with views out to Blencathra, St Johns in the Vale and Skiddaw. It has 17 bedrooms with crisp white sheets, contemporary interiors and glorious views. Downstairs at the award-winning *St Johns* restaurant, you can get a taste of the finest Lake District produce with four-course seasonal menus. For something a little more casual, head to their bar-restaurant for pub classics and plenty of local beers. There's even a *Lakeland Produce Store*, so you can stock up on local goods to take home (or on your next walk).

*Thirlspot, Thirlmere, near Keswick, CA12 4TN*
*akedistrictinns.co.uk/kings-head*

## MOUNTAIN CABIN (KIP HIDEAWAYS)

We may have had to take a breather halfway through the 30-minute ascent up a windy hill to this off-grid cabin, but the journey is absolutely worth it. Lovingly built by hand, this two-person cabin is perched high in the remote wilds just outside Cockermouth, with only a few bleating sheep for company. Every detail is as thoughtful as the last, from the brass taps above the butler's sink and the tiled shower (yes, tiled shower) to the toasty wood-burning stove, cosy, quilt-topped bed and giant window overlooking the rolling valley and navy lakes below. This place gives you all the secluded beauty of wild camping, but with all the luxuries of a boutique B&B. We spent our time there wrapped up on the outdoor chairs, sipping red wine while our pizzas crisped up in the outdoor Ooni oven (passata and olive oil provided, of course), falling asleep to utter silence with a still-blue night sky outside. If there were ever a place to escape the chaos of city life, it's this.

*Secret address provided prior to arrival, approximately 20 minutes from Keswick | kiphideaways.com | @kiphideaways*

*Mountain Cabin*

# EXPLORE

## WANDER: KESWICK TOWN

This busy market town stands in the shadows of mountains like Skiddaw
and Cat Bells, and is a good place to stop for a little re-fuelling. Wander
around the cobbled streets to find antique shops, little galleries and
plenty of friendly cafés. Call in at *Keswick Bookshop* for sun-faded antique
copies of classic gardening and art books, and fill a basket with local
cheeses and real ales at *Keswick Cheese Deli*. Try lunch at *Merienda*,
a cosy restaurant with linen-topped lights and suspended branches.
They serve simple lunches like seasonal soup and sandwiches, and
more homemade cake than any fellwalker could desire. I'll always have
a fondness for Keswick, as it furnished me with some very good walking
shoes when all I had were the fraying plimsolls on my feet.

## WANDER: GRANGE IN BORROWDALE

Four miles (6.4km) from Keswick, this storybook spot is the perfect
pitstop for a dose of English village life (and something sweet, obviously).
The famous double-arched bridge was built in 1675, and draws you into
a snoozy village like outstretched arms. The houses here are dwarfed
by the hills behind, and down by the stream ducks paddle past banks
filled with buttercups. Just beyond is the 'Jaws of Borrowdale', a dramatic
gorge leading to a lush spread of pastures surrounded by mountains.
Before exploring, though, it's probably best you get yourself to *Grange
Bridge Cottage Tea Shop*, a dolls house of a café with tables perched beside
the River Derwent. This is where we ordered two piping hot slices of
homemade cherry pie with cream and a giant pot of tea while the cyclists
at the next table geared up to tackle the next peak.

## SHOP: MARKET DAY

Pick up some freshly baked bread, preserves, condiments, seasonal
produce and artisan gin at this celebrated outdoor market in Keswick
town centre (Thursdays from February to December, and Saturdays
all year round). Award-winning food and drink, as well as trinkets and
artworks made by locals. You can eat your way along the stalls from
Market Square all the way down to Bank Street, so it's best to come late
morning or lunchtime to make the most of the goods on offer. This
market has been running for well over 700 years, and is a great way to
get a feel of the friendly Keswick spirit.

## SEE: CASTLERIGG STONE CIRCLE

As far as archeological sites go, this one must be up there with the most dramatic. Standing on a natural plateau with a backdrop of High Seat and Helvellyn, this Neolithic stone circle was one of the first in Britain, constructed in around 3000 BC. For a good circular walk of around 2 hours, start in Keswick Market Square and return via Spring Woods. You'll reach the stone circle via an old railway path.

*Castle Lane, Keswick, CA12 4RN*

## SEE: THE LINGHOLM ESTATE

You'll find this rambling country estate on the western shore of Derwentwater. It's a popular spot for walkers, who pass through for Cumbrian-roasted coffee and cake on their way to Keswick or Copperheap Bay. Beatrix Potter spent her summers here, dreaming up the story of Peter Rabbit in the estate's verdant gardens. In fact, Mr McGregor's Garden is said to be loosely based on the Lingholm Kitchen Garden, beside what is now the estate's bustling all-day restaurant serving locally-sourced food alongside artisan bakes (which are all made in the Lingholm Bakery). Once you've sampled a few local sweet treats, head to the Walled Garden for heady rose bushes, vegetable patches and a tiled, sweet-smelling greenhouse.

*Lingholm Lodge, Portinscale, Keswick, CA12 5TZ*
*thelingholmestate.co.uk | @thelingholmestate*

## SEE: THIRLMERE

We parked on the road beside the dense forest to get to Thirlmere Valley's gaping reservoir. The forest itself is thick with tall trees and ferns, and opens out on the banks of the water. There are steep fells on every side, with Helvellyn looming over its eastern edge. To the south, Dunmail Raise supposedly marks the line between north and south of the Lake District. It's a lovely place to be at dusk, when the sun turns the water a dramatically deep blue. But don't be tempted to slip in – Thirlmere is one of just a handful of places you can't swim. Probably why it stays so deliciously quiet.

*Above and below:* The Lingholm Estate, Cat Bells

## WALK: NOBLE KNOTT

This circular stroll takes you through a lush woodland brimming with flowers, pine trees and wild birds. It's a great choice if you're planning a picnic, as it's nice and short (around an hour in total) with plenty of streams – the perfect spot for an outdoor lunch on a warm day. You can park at Noble Knott car park, 4 miles (6.5km) west of Keswick and not far from the village of Braithwaite.

*Starting point: Noble Knott car park, CA12 5TW*

## WALK: CAT BELLS

For a fairly easy hike with maximum reward, climb up Cat Bells fell. Take the fairly steep zig-zaggy ascent up the face of Skelgill Bank. Once you reach the peak, you can enjoy the views (and a breather) overlooking mountain ranges and shores of Derwentwater. After that, you can either descend south down to Hawes Gate, or spin around and go back down the bank. There are opportunities for a scramble, but otherwise it's best to stick to the pathway. Climbing to the top and back will take you around an hour (depending on how long you want to sit at the top), while the Hawes Gates descent is around 2½ hours.

*You can park for free on the roadside, starting your walk from: CA12 5UE*

## WALK: HELVELLYN FROM THIRLMERE

From the summit of Helvellyn (once your heart rate returns to normal), you can see across the mighty Skiddaw mountain range. While you could choose the routes that require scrambling on the eastern side of the mountain, this one is much easier – just the way we like it. Begin at Swirls car park, south of Legburthwaite, and follow the Helvellyn Gill path for a straight up-and-down walk that will take you around 3½ hours. For a longer loop (5-ish hours) you can carry on over Nethermost Pike and Dollywaggon, come down Raise Beck to Dunmail Raise and return.

*Starting point: Swirls car park, CA12 4TW*

## WALK: RANNERDALE

If you're visiting in the spring, don't miss the incredible display of bluebells that wash across Rannerdale's 'secret valley'. Rannerdale Knotts sits between Buttermere and Crummock Water, with signs of ancient settlements dating back to the Stone Age. It's a place of soothing peace and quiet, with spectacular views from the summit. For an easy circular walk of around 2 hours, start in Buttermere village (there's plenty of parking there if you're coming by car).

*Starting point: Buttermere car park, CA13 9XA*

## WALK: LOWESWATER

For a forest walk that will take you around 2 hours, park at Maggie's Bridge to start this stroll around Loweswater. Overlooked by the enormous Blake Fell, there is either a flat walk that takes you through the forest and along the water's edge – or if you want something a bit more strenuous you can follow the track to High Nook Farm and on to High Nook Tarn and the Holme Force Waterfall. Look out for the Holme Wood Bothy, a 'stone tent' with its own log burner right on the shore. The calm waters are pretty irresistible for a swim on a warm summer's day, and are a favourite for paddleboarders and kayakers. For a similar walk with a pub finish, see page 24.

*Starting point: Maggie's Bridge car park, CA13 0RU*

## SWIM: DERWENTWATER

Just a 10-minute stroll from Keswick centre, the Cat Bells fells rise up from the west of the expansive local lake, where swimmers like to leap from Ashness jetty. With a path hugging almost all of the shoreline, Derwentwater has great access to open water for swimmers (and is particularly lovely at sunset) – although it's worth keeping an eye on the boat timetable and checking which areas are protected nature spots for the local wildlife. A loop of the water on foot is a friendly 8 miles (12.8km), making it a lovely spot for an afternoon walk – or setting up a picnic to watch canoers slice through the water.

## SWIM: BLACK MOSS POT, LANGSTRATH BECK

The fabled Black Moss Pot might just become your favourite wild swimming spot, providing you can find it. Walk 2 miles (3.2km) up to Blea Rock from Stonethwaite village (just south of Keswick) through the Langstrath Valley to find this deep, clear water. There are high rocks for jumping off and a staggered waterfall at one end, which proved itself as the perfect place to bathe away the afternoon. You won't want to leave, so be sure to bring some snacks with you.

## SWIM: BUTTERMERE

Right by the main car park in the centre of Buttermere, behind the *Bridge Hotel*, this beautiful lake is not so great for inexperienced swimmers. It has some steep underwater shelving along its edges, so only swim here if you are happy heading straight into the middle where the waters are deeper.

*Nearest postcode for Buttermere car park: CA13 9XA*

*Thirlmere*

*Honister Pass*

## SWIM: CRUMMOCK WATER

Often outshone by the next door Buttermere, this equally stunning (and actually, much bigger) lake, 12 miles (19.3km) west of Keswick, is well worth a visit. The surrounding fellsides are shot through with pine trees and blue Skiddaw slate, and you can swim with the mountains of Mellbrook to the east and Grassmoor to the west. Down by the shore, there's the meditative sound of lapping water, and you'll find sheep watching from up on a rock, and an urge to dive in despite the cold wind, or a mossy rock to just sit. Not too shabby for an early morning swim – even better when you strip down on a pine-scented shore with no one around for miles (or so we hoped). There are plenty of places to park along the B5289 tracing the edge of Crummock Water towards Buttermere.

## BIKE: WHINLATTER FOREST

An excellent place to flex your mountain biking muscles or strap on your walking shoes. This mountain forest has some seriously exhilarating views across Bassenthwaite Lake, Keswick and Derwentwater. As far as cycling trails, the *Gorse Trail* is a 6¼-mile (9.5-km) stretch along mostly well-paved ground (good for those less-balanced cyclists among us), while the *Altura Trail* is for the pros, taking you off-road 1600ft (488 metres) above Keswick – with well-deserved views at the top. It's best to book in advance for your mountain bike hire from Cyclewise Whinlatter at Whinlatter Forest Trailhead.

*cyclewise.co.uk*

## FORAGE: WHINLATTER FOREST

You'll probably be eating a lot of lovely local produce on your trip. If you're curious about where it all comes from, join a professional forager for the day to get to know the Lakes up close and personal. You'll meet the local host in Whinlatter and set off on a walk, identifying wild foods and getting to know some local edible species (plus any lookalikes) along the way. After that, you'll cook a two-course feast using all the ingredients from the day.

*notintheguidebooks.com | @notintheguidebooks*

### DRINK: LORTON VILLAGE SHOP

Just the place you want to see when you're looking for a coffee fix. Set beside a field in sleepy High Lorton, this 'shed with a view' serves an excellent flat white. You can also pick up artisan bread, local meats and vegan chocolate while you're there. Expect a chat with cyclists perched on the steps, sipping espresso and recharging before hitting the hills.

*High Lorton, Cockermouth, CA13 9UL | @lortonvillageshop*

### DRINK: THE LAKES DISTILLERY

Not far from Bassenthwaite Lake near Cockermouth, The Lakes Distillery has been making whisky since 2014 using water from Sprinkling Tarn. Their whisky-maker Dhavall Gandhi takes a holistic approach, creating spirits inspired by the Lakes themselves. You can take a tour of the distillery (formerly a derelict Victorian farmstead), followed by a heady tasting session. As well as beautiful whiskies, the site itself is worth the trip – you can even meet the alpacas that roam the grounds.

*Setmurthy, near Bassenthwaite Lake, CA13 9SJ*
*lakesdistillery.com | @lakesdistillery*

### STARGAZE: BORROWDALE VALLEY

If you live in a city like us, it may have been a while since you last saw a sky full of stars, which makes it so much more magical when you are confronted with the kind of skies you find in the Lakes. There are a lot of perfect spots for stargazing in the National Park, but this one might be our favourite. The Borrowdale Valley stretches south from Derwentwater. It is home to the winding Honister Pass leading down into the Buttermere Valley, as well as the soaring Scafell Pike which sits proudly at its southern end. Jump in the car and go uphill, safely pulling over as far away from any light sources as you can. The skies up here are deep and dark, and on a clear night the Milky Way puts on a stunning show for you.

### DRIVE: HONISTER PASS

To take in the dramatic surroundings without getting a blister, hop in the car to follow this jaw-dropping mountain pass connecting the Buttermere and Borrowdale valleys. Beginning at Seatoller, around 7 miles (11km) from Keswick, the road is at an elevation of 1167ft (356 metres) and snakes through the valley for just under 4 miles (6km). There are a few narrow (read: hairy) bits where reversing skills are handy. But it's worth it to meander through the mountains on a clear day, with dry stone walls leading the way and the clouds making shadows on the fells.

# ESKDALE, WASTWATER AND NEARBY

# ESKDALE, WASTWATER AND NEARBY

These two valleys are on the western side of the Lake
District, not far from the sea. This area is far more remote
and less popular with holidaymakers, captivating those in
search of peace. Wastwater is the deepest lake in the country,
with looming scree slopes plunging into the water and a 3-mile
(4.8km) south-facing shoreline of volcanic quartz. The water is
uncannily clear thanks to the lack of sediment from the quartz,
and you'll find tiny bays along the shore calling out for picnics.
The whole place is overlooked by mighty Scafell Pike. Climb
a little and you'll find some excellent high-level swims, with epic
views down to Derwentwater. Carve out a day to explore these
valleys, which cry out for wild swims, mountain climbs and
starry-skied wild camping.

# EAT

## BOWER HOUSE INN

Get your pub grub fix at this romantic little coaching inn, tucked between Mitredale and Muncaster Fell. It's been feeding walkers for over 250 years, and is a good place to end up after tackling nearby Scafell Pike. It has 20 bedrooms if you need somewhere cosy to stay, and there's a beer garden for sunnier days. The food is classic and comforting. Think creamy chicken and leek pie, scampi and chips or steak and ale pie, best finished with a bowl of hot apple crumble.

*Eskdale, Holmrook, West Lakes, CA19 1TD*
*bowerhouseinn.com | @bowerhouseinn*

## THE BOOT INN

Another Cumbrian inn with all the warmth of a freshly baked pie. Dishes are chalked up in the bar, with satisfying stuff like Cumberland sausage and mash, fish and chips or five bean vegan chilli on offer. There's a beer garden out the back too.

*Eskdale, CA19 1TG | thebooteskdale.co.uk*

## WOOLPACK INN

This historic inn at the base of the Hardknott Pass does all the classics using local produce, and there's a pizza oven churning out piping hot, mozzarella-laden slices all day. There's a handful of lovely rooms, too.

*Hardknott Pass, Eskdale, CA19 1TH | woolpack.co.uk*

## WASDALE HEAD INN AND CAMPSITE

Proudly calling itself 'the home of British rock climbing', this is the only hotel in the Wasdale Valley – just north of Wastwater and a 9-minute drive from Ritson's Force. It's a legendary pub for hikers tackling the local fells, serving generous comfort food (including local Herdwick lamb). Buried in the hills, the giant 'INN' sign on its side is a bit of a mirage after a tough day's climbing. Expect simple, clean rooms with comfy beds and classic breakfasts included.

*Wasdale Head, Gosforth, CA20 1EX | wasdale.com*

# EXPLORE

## WALK: STYHEAD AND SPRINKLING TARNS

This circular walk takes you through some of the highest and most rugged of the Lakeland fells. Styhead and Sprinkling tarns lie at the end of the twin valleys at the tip of Borrowdale. Both have still, clear water and are hugged by the rock faces of Great Gable (Styhead) and Great End (Sprinkling). Start at Seathwaite and head up Grains Gill, returning via Styhead Tarn. The walk will take you less than 3 hours, depending on whether you brave the cold waters along the way. Which, we must admit, we didn't...

*Starting point: Seathwaite car park, CA12 5XJ*

## WALK: WOOLPACK TO HARDKNOTT ROMAN FORT

Set aside a couple of hours for this walk, which starts at the car park beside Jubilee Bridge at the bottom of Hardknott Pass. Once you've started ascending the hill, look out for signs for Hardknott Fort (*english-heritage.org.uk*). This remote Roman fort was built under Hadrian's rule in the 2nd century, and you can still find the remains of the stone bath house and headquarters. The views from here are phenomenal – on a clear day, you can see all the way down to the coast and the sweeping Eskdale Horseshoe. If you don't fancy the walk, it's also possible to drive here via the famous Hardknott Pass road (see page 34).

*Starting point: Jubilee Bridge car park, CA19 1TH*

## WALK: SCAFELL PIKE

The mother of the Lake District's mountains. England's highest peak reaches 3209ft (978 metres), and is the pinnacle of Lake District hikes. It's a challenging ascent, but actually very doable for most people. Carve out around 7 hours for your round trip, and arm yourself with plenty of snacks. The easiest way (take 'easiest' with a pinch of salt here) is from Wasdale head hamlet, while routes from Borrowdale or Eskdale will take a little longer on rougher mountain terrain. Either way, you can look forward to breathtaking views across the Lakes and beyond. They're enough to turn anyone into a Romantic poet.

*Nearest postcodes for parking at: Wasdale head hamlet, CA20 1EX; Borrowdale, CA12 5UP; Eskdale Green, CA19 1TX*

## WALK: RITSON'S FORCE

To get to this series of hammering waterfalls in the beautiful Mosedale Valley, cross the bridge from the garden of the Wasdale Head Inn in Gosforth, situated between the Eskdale Valley and the western Lakes region, and wander up the track through the field (before, or after, stopping for a pick-me-up at the pub). The walk will take you through the lush valley, with excellent views of Scafell and Scafell Pike. You'll soon see signs for Ritson's Force (good old National Trust), and you'll reach the falls by going through the gate and downhill towards the peaceful woodlands. The walk will take around half an hour. We recommend taking a blanket and lying on the grassy hillside next to the waterfall, for some sunny afternoon reading with a soundtrack of falling water.

*Starting point: Wasdale Head Inn, Gosforth, CA20 1EX*

## WALK: BLACK COMBE

This head-spinning walk is a tough one, so only do it if you're up for a long walk and plenty of climbing. Rising up from the sea at the far south-west corner of the Lake District, Black Combe is one of the Lake District's most spectacular peaks. It stands at 2000ft (610 metres) on its south-west edge. At the summit, the views seem to go on forever – in fact, it's said you can see up to 14 counties from the top. It's a big climb, but the path up is clear and easy to follow. From St Anne's Church in Thwaites, cross the A595 and follow the paths to the farm over Baystone Bank. Following the lane, you'll take a right turn through the gate, turning left by the wall. After that, the base of Black Combe is easy to find. To make the most of the views, try and do this walk on a clear, sunny day (if possible). The soft golden light across the fells is unforgettable.

*Starting point: St Anne's Church, Thwaites, LA18 5HP*

## SWIM: TONGUE POT, ESKDALE

It's a fairly strenuous walk up here, starting at the bottom of Hardknott Pass (on the same side as the Roman fort). Walk the track up the valley and follow the River Esk until you reach a fork. Tongue Pot is for the more daring swimmers among us, with jumps of up to 16½-ft (5-m) deep waters. It is one of a cluster of sparkling pools, with smaller (and shallower) pools above it and the more secluded Kail Pot below. This one 4-ft (1.2-m) deep, is more tranquil and catches the most sunlight.

## SWIM AND WALK: GREENDALE FALLS

Plunge into the deep pools of this south-facing gill in the hamlet of Greendale. You'll see the path up the fell, and ¼ mile (400m) up is where you'll find the sparkling waterfall, with the tarn another mile (1.6km) up. For a lovely walk, continue north towards Greendale Valley towards the summit of Middle Fell. You'll get stunning views over the Wasdale screes (loose stones across the mountain slope) and western fells.

*Nearest postcode for parking along the road: CA20 IEU*

## CYCLE: THE ESKDALE TRAIL

Set off from Dalegarth Station (CA19 ITG) on a fairly easy 2-hour cycle (apart from Chapel Hill, a ¾ mile (1.2km) steep ascent that we pushed our bikes up) that'll take you through ancient Eskdale Valley woodland and riverside meadows, finishing in the coastal village of Ravenglass – the only seaside village in the national park. Be sure to stop for an ice cream in Boot on your way, and on a summer's day you can cool off with a swim at Forge Bridge. To get back to Dalegarth, jump on the Ravenglass and Eskdale Railway with your bike, but please note you must pre-book your bike onto the train. If you don't have your own, hire a bike from close to Dalegarth station (*westlakesadventure.co.uk/hire*).

*ravenglass-railway.co.uk*

## SEE: BURNMOOR STONE CIRCLES

There's a pretty tough (but short) walk from the village of Boot in the Eskdale Valley, leading up to these five atmospheric stone circles. They are said to be around 4000 years old, with a stone cairn marking one burial. The biggest one here is Brat's Hill, which has 42 stones. It's still not known what exactly they were for, and their mystery is of course part of the appeal. Found high on the slopes of Boat How, the site covers nearly a square mile (2.5 sq km). It's beautifully peaceful up here, with lovely views across the heathery hills.

## WANDER: ST BEES

For some sea air, drive half an hour west from Wastwater to the pretty coastal village of St Bees. Towering red sandstone cliffs look out towards the Isle of Man, and the mile-long (1.6km) stretch of sandy beach is one of the most beautiful in the area. Walk its windswept length and look out for its tidal rock pools along the way. There are a handful of classic Cumbrian pubs in the village – try *Queens Hotel* on Main Street for hearty food and friendly locals.

# GRASMERE

# GRASMERE

The resting place of William Wordsworth, this butter-hued
village is the end destination for most walkers at some point
or another along their trip. It's where you'll find some of the
most bustling restaurants and pubs – places to sink into for
pints of bitter and giant burgers. On sunny evenings, the best
place to be is the shore. Head to the banks of Thirlmere, just
a few miles up the road from Grasmere, to watch swans drifting
on the water, people trotting across the hills on horseback and
evening swimmers in pink rubber hats pull buoys across the lake.
We made a little routine of taking beers down to a particularly
secluded bit of beach after dinner each evening, wondering out
loud if we should just throw off our clothes and get in. Most
nights, I admit, we decided the water was too cold. But the view
of the peaks above the glittering water – combined with a cold
local beer – is memorable enough as it is.

*Tweedies Bar & Lodge Restaurant*

# EAT

### THE GOOD SPORT

This friendly pub on the road out of the village is always busy. And it's not hard to see why. There's a riverfront garden, and they boast 'proper coffee' and home-cooked, English pub grub all day long. But we love it most for the beer and cider, which is all brewed by hand at Lake View Farm and comes fresh from the taps. The perfect place for a post-hike pint.

*1 Stock Lane, Grasmere, Ambleside, LA22 9SJ | grasmerepub.com*
*@goodsportgrasmere*

### GRASMERE TEA GARDENS

There's no shortage of sweet things to eat in Grasmere. Join hungry hikers for scones, freshly baked cakes, doorstep sandwiches and tea in china cups at this lovely little place, which has a waterside patio overlooking the River Rothay.

*Church Bridge/Stock La, Ambleside, LA22 9SN*
*facebook.com/GrasmereTeaGardens*

### BALDRY'S

For buttery toast, jam and big mugs of tea, there's no better place than this traditional tearoom in the village. Get a seat outside on a warm day to watch the walkers pass by, and don't miss the supersize scones, which come with the obligatory pots of butter, cream and strawberry jam.

*Red Lion Square, Grasmere, Ambleside, LA22 9SP*
*baldrysgrasmere.com | @baldrysgrasmere*

### TWEEDIES BAR AND LODGE RESTAURANT

With its flagstone floors, classic banquet seats and sage-coloured walls, the bar and restaurant of *Tweedies Lodge* (see page 72) is exactly where you want to be after a long day of walking. They serve seasonal comfort food bursting with flavour, plus local ale (naturally) and interesting wines. It has all the loud, welcoming trappings of a classic country pub, but with some of the best food in the area.

*Red Bank Road, Grasmere, Ambleside, LA22 9SW*
*tweediesgrasmere.com | @tweediesbar*

## MATHILDE'S

Named after the young Norwegian woman who fell in love with the painter Alfred Heaton Cooper (whose gallery is adjoining), this bright and airy café is the perfect spot to start the day. High ceilings, wooden floors, giant glass doors and an outdoor terrace in the shadow of the hills, it serves perfect flat whites and Scandinavian-inspired breakfasts and lunches. Many of the dishes are of the 'husmanskost' ('farmers' food') variety – slow-cooked beef and crispy onions on Viking rye; meatballs with mash and sauerkraut; mackerel pâté with pickled rhubarb. For breakfast, try their homemade granola with skyr – and maybe a bloody mary to start the day right.

*Heaton Cooper Studio, Grasmere, Ambleside, LA22 9SX*
*heatoncooper.co.uk | @mathildesgrasmere*

## LUCIA'S COFFEE + BAKEHOUSE

If there's a better cinnamon bun in the Lake District, we want to know about it. This breezy café is all blue tiles and stripped wood, with an open bakery at the back. It's almost impossible to choose between their flaky sausage rolls, sourdough sandwiches and golden cheese pasties, but whatever you choose, just make sure you get yourself one of those cinnamon buns; fluffy, sticky dough slick with spiced sugar and butter. Best served fresh from the oven along with a cup of locally-roasted Redbank coffee.

*College St, Grasmere, Ambleside, LA22 9SY*
*facebook.com/luciascoffeeandbakehouse | @luciascoffeeandbakehouse*

## FOREST SIDE

It's pretty hard to get a table at this award-winning, critically acclaimed restaurant inside a gothic mansion. If you book ahead, you can feast on four- or six-course tasting menus that celebrate the rich produce and varied landscape of the Lake District, from hand-picked vegetables to locally reared meats, and fruit from the trees within the grounds. They pair every intricate, artful dish with wines from biodynamic and organic vineyards – chosen by their very own sommelier. Rooms are also available, and judging by the comfortable formality of the dining room, they'll definitely be worth the splurge.

*Keswick Road, Grasmere, Ambleside, LA22 9RN*
*theforestside.com | @the_forest_side*

*Clockwise from top left*: Mathilde's, Forest Side,
Forest Side, Tweedies Bar and Lodge Restaurant

# SLEEP

### TWEEDIES BAR AND LODGE

This family-run hotel is set in a sprawling country house in the centre of Grasmere. Downstairs it's all cosy sofas, roaring fires and a dining room leading onto a lawn, while upstairs the rooms are finished in soothing shades of navy and green, with huge beds, tartan touches and sash windows. We arrived on a rainy afternoon and collapsed straight into the squishy sofas in their living room. Coffee came in a metal pot, the perfect partner for the bag of still-warm gingerbread we'd bought next door. Plus they serve some of the best food in the region (see page 69).

*Red Bank Road, Grasmere, Ambleside, LA22 9SW*
*tweediesgrasmere.com | @tweediesbar*

### THE YAN

A great central option near Grasmere, this family-run boutique hotel and bistro on Broadrayne Farm is dramatically tucked between two fells with a sweeping view over Grasmere. A great starting point for lots of beautiful walks around Ambleside, you'll return to clean spacious rooms with comfy beds and the beloved Bistro downstairs which offers everything a hungry fell-walker could crave – from seafood sharing platters to their famous cottage pie. The adjacent farmhouse dates back to the 17th century. The Yan is well set up for outdoor adventurers, packed lunches are available – plus a drying room for muddy shoes and kit, and bike storage. If you want to bring your dog, it is a small extra fee.

*Broadrayne Farm, Grasmere, Ambleside, LA22 9RU*
*theyan.co.uk | @yanatbroadrayne*

### GRASMERE GLAMPING

Another option at Broadrayne Farm, these two luxury glamping pods are hand-built and well equipped with everything you might need for a Lake District getaway. Log-burning stoves, plus fully equipped kitchens with an oven, induction hob and small fridge mean you can cater for yourself – if you can tear yourself away from on-site restaurant *The Yan*. This doesn't even come close to camping, with underfloor heating, smart TVs and fresh linen – another perfect option if you want to unwind amongst nature for a while (with all your creature comforts intact).

*Broadrayne Farm, Grasmere, Ambleside, LA22 9RU*
*grasmereglamping.co.uk | @grasmereglamping*

*The Yan*

*Grasmere Gingerbread Shop*

# EXPLORE

### SHOP: SAM READ BOOKSELLER

Disappear into this award-winning independent bookshop, a creaky-floored haven that's been serving Grasmere since 1887. Pick up classic love letters to the local area, extensive walking and wildlife guides, Romantic poetry (of course) and an excellent selection of contemporary fiction. You can never have enough books, after all.

*Broadgate House, Grasmere, Ambleside, LA22 9SY*
*samreadbooks.co.uk | @samreadbookseller*

### SHOP: GRASMERE GINGERBREAD SHOP

We didn't know we were searching for 'the world's best gingerbread' until it was in front of us. But this beloved cottage-turned-shop sells giant stacks of golden, crumbly slices every day. The shop's third-generation owners still use the original recipe first invented by Grasmere local Sarah Nelson in 1854. Queues trail round the corner into the churchyard, with the sweet, spicy smell of baking in the air. Gingerbread comes hot and fresh, wrapped in printed paper and slipped into a brown paper bag.

*Church Cottage, Grasmere, Ambleside, LA22 9SW*
*grasmeregingerbread.co.uk | @grasmeregingerbread*

### SEE: HEATON COOPER STUDIO

Pay this little gallery a visit after you've filled up on flat whites and rye at *Mathilde's* café next door (see page 70). Alfred Heaton Cooper and his son William were both influential artists celebrating the beauty and spirituality of the local landscape through their brushes. William was an authority on the geology of the area, rendering the landscape in meticulous detail. This studio is made up of three galleries showing the art of the Heaton Cooper family, with exhibitions on throughout the year and an excellent art shop if you're feeling inspired.

*Heaton Cooper Studio, Grasmere, Ambleside, LA22 9SX*
*heatoncooper.co.uk | @heatoncooperstudio*

### SEE: SOUR MILK GHYLL WATERFALL

This frothy waterfall flows from Bleaberry tarn right down to Buttermere. It's a soothing place to come and sit if you like the sound of cascading water – and there are lots of smooth rocks around to perch on. You can reach the waterfall easily from Grasmere village, with glorious views of the lake, Haystacks and Fleetwith Pike as you walk up to it. Visit in the late afternoon to avoid the crowds and enjoy it in total peace.

## WALK: HELM CRAG

This much-loved walk takes you northwest of Grasmere village, starting on Easedale Road. It's an exhilarating 4-mile (6.5-km) walk, and the rocks of the southeast summit are known as 'The Lion and Lamb' by locals. 'The Old Lady Playing the Organ' is at the other end of the ridge, and is a far trickier climb.

*Starting point: Easedale Road, LA22 9QH*

## STARGAZING: ALLAN BANK

Another favourite stargazing spot for deprived city folk like us. Allan Bank is one of just two recognised 'Dark Sky Discovery Sites' in Cumbria. Allan Bank is a two-storey Georgian villa perched high on a hill, hugged by woodland to the west of Grasmere village. It was once the home of William Wordsworth, so is a popular spot for visitors during the day. In the evening, there is barely any light disturbance here, making it the perfect spot to stop and take in the stars. You might even catch a meteor shower if you stand in this dark, wild spot long enough.

*Grasmere, Ambleside, LA22 9QB*

## PICNIC: EASEDALE TARN

In true Cumbrian style, pack some cheese, bread and beer and walk 5 miles (8km) from Grasmere village to this glorious tarn. The walk is nice and simple, and there's no better way to end it than by settling down beside the water for a little alfresco feast. You'll also have the pleasure of passing the frothy waters of Sour Milk Ghyll (not the most appetising of names, it has to be said) on your way up to the tarn (see page 75).

## WALK AND SWIM: RYDAL WATER

Arm yourself with a pocket full of gingerbread and either park up the hill by the church in Rydal village, or at Pelter Bridge or White Moss car parks. From any of these, it's a short and leisurely walk towards this serene lake – one of the smallest but prettiest of them all (just ask Wordsworth, he lived on Rydal Mount overlooking the water). Take the high path beside River Rothay for views down to the water as you stroll above the southern shore. We came later in the day, settling down on the banks with a cold beer to watch swimmers slice through the water in the evening sun. It's a mile (1.6km) long and relatively shallow compared to neighbouring tarns, so it warms up nicely in the summer. There are smooth rocks to climb into the water from (or sunbathe on), too.

*Nearest postcode for parking at the church: LA22 9LR*

*Rydal Water*

# PENRITH
# AND
# NEARBY

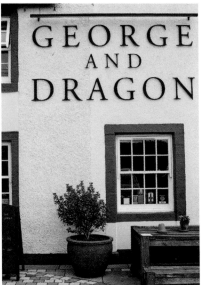

# PENRITH AND NEARBY

The gateway to the Eden Valley and North Pennines, Penrith
is a little more industrial-feeling than its sibling towns. But no
less charming once you dig in. In fact, its position just outside
the national park means it's often overlooked by visitors and has
retained its old spirit over the years. Undulating across a series of
hilly streets and alleyways, it's brimming with lovely places to
eat, drink and be merry, with a bustling market on Tuesdays.
As for nature, the northeastern fells are within easy reach, while
Ullswater is just down the road.

# EAT

## GEORGE AND DRAGON

We popped in here for a quick half pint and ended up staying for a 2-hour long lunch, which says a lot about how inviting this pub 3 miles (5km) from Penrith is. Most of the menu is made using this home-reared produce, and anything else comes from farms within 20 miles (32km) of the pub. Their food is 'classic country cooking', with contemporary twists here and there. The frosty copper taps at the bar pump out real Cumbrian ales, and there's a great wine list too. A top choice for visitors wanting to spend the night in Penrith, they have individually-decorated rooms, too.

*Clifton, Penrith, CA10 2ER | georgeanddragonclifton.co.uk*
*@georgeanddragonclifton*

## FOUR AND TWENTY

This light and airy bistro in a former bank describes their food as 'flavourful and unfussy drawing on seasonal British cooking'. Four and Twenty offers a set menu of two courses. If you're vegan or vegetarian, get in touch ahead of your visit and they'll prepare something special for you.

*42 King Street, Penrith, CA11 7AY | fourandtwentypenrith.co.uk*
*@four_and_twenty_*

## THE DOG AND GUN INN

This gastropub churns out consistently delicious dishes, from West Coast crab tarts with pickled radish and grapefruit hollandaise to grass-fed beef shin with charred hispi cabbage, roast mushroom and truffle. They proudly source from local suppliers, including fish from Maryport, corn-fed chicken from Lancashire and veg from Embleton. We love settling in by the fire with a glass of wine, with a portion of triple-cooked chips on the way.

*Skelton, Penrith, CA11 9SE*
*dogandgunskelton.co.uk | @dog_and_gun_skelton*

## THE CHOPPING BLOCK PENRITH

Pop into this butcher, deli and café for elevated classics like French toast and classic cheese burgers with dill pickles. This small team is genuinely passionate about what they do. Stock up on great British cheeses, cured meats, artisanal condiments and Fell Brewery beers (made in Grange-over-Sands). As for the meat, they won 2020's 'UK's Best New Butchery' award, so whether you're after Herdwick lamb from the Cumbrian fells or heritage pork from the Southern Lakes, they've got you covered.

*5 Two Lions Square, New Squares, Penrith, CA11 7FX*
*thechoppingblockpenrith.com | @choppingblockpenrith*

*George and Dragon*

# EXPLORE

## SHOP: BRUNSWICK YARD

Get lost browsing the antique ceramics, books, glassware and furniture at this bustling antiques salvage yard moments from Penrith market square. Most of the wares have been sourced locally, so it's a great place to find a few gifts (for yourself or otherwise). *The Yard Kitchen* is the on-site café, selling Carvetii coffee, organic Storm tea and seasonal brunches, lunches and bakes. You'll also find a lovingly-organised record shop, *Withnail Books* and *Brunswick Rugs of Asia*. Tucked inside the arches of the market is Sam Jary, the biodynamic viticulturist behind *Black Hand Wine*. Sam makes 'honest' wine for Cumbrian tables and beyond, travelling to France each year to produce the finest wine with the least intervention. He poured us a glass of his zippy natural red while the Talking Heads danced on a projected screen above our heads.

*Brunswick Road, Penrith, CA11 7LU*
*brunswickyard.com | @thebrunswickyard*

## WALK: LACY'S CAVES AND LONG MEG CIRCULAR WALK

Carved into the red sandstone cliffs by the River Eden, these five chambers were built in the 18th century by Colonel Lacy – apparently as the perfect gathering spot for parties. The caves are definitely popular with tourists, but there's a stretch of quiet, open river that cries out for secluded swims on a hot day (or cold, depending on how brave you are). To get to the caves, park in Little Salkeld to find the footpath. You can also kayak from Langwathby, which will take you down to the little waterfalls towards the caves. On foot, the 5¼-mile (8-km) loop will take you from Little Salkeld past the mysterious Long Meg stone circle, Addingham's ancient church and the chambers of Lacy's Caves.

*Nearest postcode for parking in the village is: CA10 1NW*

*Left to right:* Brunswick Yard, Black Hand Wine

WINDEREMERE

# WINDERMERE

Even if you haven't been to the Lake District, you've probably heard
of Lake Windermere. It's a mile (1.6km) wide and 10½ miles (17-km)
long, making it the biggest body of water in England. Tourists
flock here each year for sailing, steaming and sunbathing, so
you won't be surprised to hear that Windermere town gets pretty
rammed. But don't let that put you off. There's a pride to this little
town, with plenty of classic pubs and a few excellent restaurants
to keep you busy in the evenings. Down in the busy resort area of
Bowness-on-Windermere (on the lake's eastern shore), you can
wander the jetties or hop on a steamer for a tour of the islands.

# EAT

## HOMEGROUND COFFEE + KITCHEN

Always buzzing with locals and visitors, *Homeground* feels like a bit of a Windermere institution. It has all the wood panelling, counter seating and breeziness of a classic antipodean café. The food is made from scratch. They make their sauces and preserves in-house, get their bread from local sourdough baker Lovingly Artisan and use Carvetii coffee (owners Rich and Jane's favourite roast) for flat whites and espressos.

*Main Road, Windermere, LA23 1DX*
*homegroundcafe.co.uk | @homegroundcafe*

## BREW ROOM

Fill up on strong coffee and big, home-cooked breakfasts made with artisan ingredients at this family-run café in the town centre. The all-day vegan breakfast is a good place to start, or go for the spicy Turkish eggs with avocado, eggs benedict or salmon-loaded crumpets.

*31–33 Crescent Road, Windermere, LA23 1BL*
*brew-room.co.uk | @brew.room*

## HENROCK

Simon Rogan's elegant restaurant is set in the grounds of Linthwaite House, high in the hills above Lake Windermere. The dining room is full of art, sculpture and sumptuous furniture – the perfect setting for their creative à la carte menus inspired by the chef's travels around the world. Their menu showcases the seasonal produce of the local area, grown with innovative techniques on a regenerative farm in nearby Cartmel, with a commitment to sustainability and minimal waste.

*Linthwaite House Hotel, Crook Rd, Bowness-on-Windermere, LA23 3JA*
*henrock.co.uk | @henrocksimonrogan*

## THE LITTLE ICE CREAM SHOP

There's one of these sky-blue ice cream shops in Hawkshead too (we visited both, strictly for research purposes). The queues out the door start mid-morning and continue all day long, but their slow-churned, small-batch ice cream is definitely worth the wait. They serve 22 flavours each day, and change them all the time according to season and mood. Think salted caramel, black cherry and Hawkshead gingerbread, all made with cream and milk from Cumbrian cows.

*39 Crescent Rd, Windermere, LA23 1BL*
*thelittleicecreamshop.com | @thelittleicecreamshop*

# SLEEP

### CEDAR MANOR

This family-run boutique hotel was built back in 1854, and is less than 10 minutes from Windermere town on foot. Every room is different, with colourful touches and rich tones throughout. The quiet gardens are a lovely place to relax on warm afternoons, or unwind in the living room after a day exploring the nearby lakes and mountains.

*Ambleside Road, Windermere, LA23 1AX*
*cedarmanor.co.uk | @cedarmanorhotel*

### CHURCH STREET

The Lake District is peppered with wonderful Airbnbs to stay in. This stylish two-bedroom flat is one of a few properties owned and operated by local couple Niall and Marta, who also run an interior design company (*@verdantinteriors*). The flat is conveniently located on Windermere's Church Street, and is comfortable and clean. Having lived in the Lakes their whole lives, Niall and Marta are on hand to happily give local advice.

*14 Church Street, Windermere, LA23 1AQ*
*airbnb.com/h/churchstreetwindermere*

# EXPLORE

## DRINK: THE CRAFTY BAA

While all that Cumbrian real ale is great, we'd be lying if
we said a pint of frosty craft didn't slip down very nicely.
The Crafty Baa serves a huge selection of experimental
brews in a cosy, low-lit bar on Victoria Street. Pull up
a stool and let your vanilla porter or Chicago IPA work
its magic beside the open fire.

*21 Victoria Street, Windermere, LA23 1AB*
*thecraftybaa.com | @the_crafty_baa_*

## WALK: ORREST HEAD

The summit of Orrest Head was one of the first views that
stole the heart of the famous fell walker Alfred Wainwright.
Fresh off the train from Blackburn, the 23-year-old climbed
the path up to the viewpoint at Orrest. To follow his lead,
just look out for signs for Orrest Head opposite Windermere
railway station. The walk to the top takes around an hour.
From the summit, you can see Windermere's lakes and fells,
the sky giant and gaping above it all. It's not hard to see why,
after standing looking at this very view, Wainwright went on
to commit his life to the Lake District.

## WALK AND CYCLE: GRIZEDALE FOREST

With its glittering tarns, mossy hills and sun-spun woodland,
you can spend all day ambling through Grizedale Forest.
There are plenty of walking trails to choose from, and you
can also rent a bike (Biketreks Grizedale is a good bet,
*bike-treks.co.uk*) and follow one of the seven cycling routes in
the area. Since 1977, international artists have been creating
sculptures to be dotted around the undergrowth, from
surreal artworks to pieces that slot organically into their
surroundings. There are often exhibitions and events on,
so take a look at the Grizdale Sculpture website before you
visit. You can also make use of their interactive sculpture
guide, created by art expert Edwina Fitzpatrick.

*Starting point: Grizedale Forest Visitor Centre, LA23 0QJ*
*grizedalesculpture.org | @grizedale_sculpture_*

*Windermere*

## CYCLE: COUNTRY LANES CYCLE CENTRE

This friendly bike hire shop is right next to Windermere train station, so you can hop straight on. They pride themselves on a sustainable approach to tourism that protects the sensitive landscape, so use local suppliers, recycle their products and use solar power at the hire centre. You can choose from a great range of mountain, electric or carbon road bikes. Their thoughtful cycle routes avoid fragile natural areas and busy roads, leading along peaceful country lanes with some of the best views in the area. Go solo, or check their website to join group cycle events and guided cycle rides.

*The Railway Station Precinct, Windermere, LA23 1AH*
*countrylaneslakedistrict.co.uk*

## WATCH: ROYALTY CINEMA

While it's true you'll want to spend most of your time exploring the great outdoors, this is here for you if you do fancy catching a film – and there aren't many cinemas like this around. Set in an Art Deco-era building, this place has three screens. The main one is adorned with glowing red velvet and wood panelling, with a period auditorium and Wurlitzer organ glistening in the corner.

*Lake Road North, Bowness-on-Windermere, LA23 3BJ*
*windermere.nm-cinemas.co.uk/windermere*

## SAIL: LAKELAND ADVENTURES

We like to think we have a natural knack for sailing. We just haven't tried it yet. If, like us, you love the idea of getting out on the waters of Windermere but have no idea what a gooseneck is, consider hiring someone else to do the difficult bit for you. Lakeland Adventures offers 2–6-hour chartered sailing trips for groups of up to eight people, skipper and hostess included. You can choose to get as involved with the sailing part as you like, or just sit back with a glass of wine and watch Windermere glide past.

*1 Glebe Rd, Bowness-on-Windermere, LA23 3HE*
*lakelandadventures.com*

## SEE: CLAIFE VIEWING STATION

Found in the upland area of Claife Heights, this viewing station was constructed in the 1790s. a It's a 10-minute walk from the Windermere Lake Cruises Ferry House and you can see for miles across Lake Windermere and beyond from up here. The original drawing room had different coloured glass on every window to celebrate the shades of each season and its light; autumnal orange, summery yellow, spring green and winter blue. It is the first example of a real tourist attraction in the Lakes, and has been lovingly restored by the National Trust to reflect its original magic. The station is on the western shores of Lake Windermere (there are regular cruises to the western shores from Bowness during peak season), and you can stroll from the viewing station to Ash Landing Nature Reserve to see wildflowers and butterflies or bring your bicycle on the cruise for a gentle (but very scenic) ride along the shore path.

## WANDER: NEAR SAWREY

Wander around this friendly little village for a slice of Cumbrian village life, complete with stone cottages, billowing washing lines and cows grazing in the fields. And, of course, no perfect village would be complete without the local pub. Stop at the *Tower Bank Arms* (*towerbankarms.co.uk*) for a glass of something cold and refreshing (or tepid and strong) in the cobbled, honeysuckle-scented garden.

# KENDAL
# AND
# NEARBY

# KENDAL AND NEARBY

This old market town is often referred to as the southern gateway to the Lake District. It has plenty of pretty pubs, cinemas and boutique shops – including its own 'Creative Quarter' – and is only 8 miles (13km) from Lake Windermere. The town's rich wool-making history is reflected in the local motto '*Pannus mihi panis*' ('Cloth is my bread'). It still has that old industrial feeling to it, which is all part of the charm.

# EAT

## THE BAKERY @ NO.4

Run by pastry chefs Marianne Woodend and Melissa Spencer, who worked with Simon Rogan (see page 140) and at *The Drunken Duck* (see page 110) respectively, *Bakery @ No.4* has quickly gained a reputation for having some of the best bakes in the Lake District. They create everything according to what the season has on offer, so you are guaranteed to find something interesting on the countertop each day. We loved the spiced toffee apple cake and apricot frangipane tart – and the strawberry and almond meringue cake. They also stock award-winning sourdough from local bakery *Grain*.

*40 Woolpack Yard, Kendal, LA9 4NG*
*bakery4.co.uk | @bakeryatno4*

## THE BLACK BULL

We've broken the rules a bit here by crossing over from the Lake District to the Yorkshire Dales – but only just. If you're exploring the landscape surrounding Kendal you'll want to visit this husband-and-wife-run pub 11 miles (17.5km) from the market town. Head Chef Nina Matsunaga lightly fuses classic British pub food with Japanese flavours to delicious effect – think hand-dived scallops with yuzu and wild halibut with shiso, beef tartare with Thai basil and tea leaves, and banoffee pie with peanut. There is a focus on using local produce, native breeds sourced from no more than 20 miles (32km) away, and sustainably sourced fish from the North Sea and local freshwater fish. Plus eclectic wines and locally brewed beers – with rooms available too.

*44 Main Street, Sedbergh, LA10 5BL*
*theblackbullsedbergh.co.uk | @theblackbullsedbergh*

*The Black Bull*

## COMIDA

Locals flock to this friendly neighbourhood tapas bar, run by Andalusian Alba and Yorkshireman Simon. Settle in for jamon croquettes, *mojama* (air-dried tuna loin from Andalusia with tomato) and patatas bravas with hot paprika aioli. These are some of their signatures, but there are a good selection of vegetarian and vegan dishes too. Don't miss the award-winning Spanish beer made with seawater, and be sure to save room for a slice of the burnt Basque cheesecake. You can also pop in for brunch at the weekend.

*90–92 Highgate, Kendal, LA9 4HE | comidafood.co.uk | @comida_kendal*

## TEBAY SERVICES

After the M6 motorway was built through their farm 16 miles (26km) north of Kendal, John and Barbara Dunning opened Tebay Services as the UK's first family-run service station. What started in 1972 as a small 40-seat restaurant with a small local craft shop has now grown into a sprawling mega-deli, a butchers and a farmshop stocking goods from 70 local producers within a 30-mile (48-km) radius. In the kitchen, they use Cumbrian lamb and native beef raised on the farm for their pies and Sunday lunches, while the coffee is roasted less than 30 miles (48km) away in the northern Lake District.

*Westmorland Place, Orton, Penrith, CA10 3SB*
*tebayservices.com | @tebayservices*

*Above and below:* Tebay Services

*Clockwise from top left: The Little Ice Cream Shop, Hawkshead Brewery,
The Beatrix Potter Gallery, Hawkshead Brewery*

# EXPLORE

### ARTS: BREWERY ARTS CENTRE

Head to this vibrant Arts Centre in the creative heart of Kendal for film, music and great food. They have live gigs, theatre and art events all year round, showcasing some of the best talent in Cumbria and beyond. There are two screening rooms, complete with classic red velvet chairs, and you can take a beer in with you.

*122A Highgate, Kendal, LA9 4HE | breweryarts.co.uk | @brewery_arts_kendal*

### DRINK: HAWKSHEAD BREWERY

You'll notice this beer in bars and restaurants all over the area, but the best place to taste it is straight from the tap. This is Hawkshead Brewery's tap bar, serving their refreshing 'beer from the Lakes' in an airy brewery and beer hall in the village of Staveley, 5 miles (8km) north of Kendal (they moved location from close to Hawkshead back in 2006). Stop by for everything from classic lagers and hazy pints to tiramisu stouts and great alcohol-free brews. They have also partnered up with *More?*, the artisan bakery next door, so you can settle in for a pizza and beer session (the perfect rainy afternoon activity, we say).

*14 Back Lane, Staveley, Kendal, LA8 9LR | hawksheadbrewery.co.uk @hawksheadbrewery*

# AMBLESIDE
# AND NEARBY

# AMBLESIDE AND NEARBY

This compact town on the western shores of Lake Windermere is another great place to use as a base. There's no shortage of places to eat and drink, and it's overlooked by the Langdale Pikes. Many walkers use the town as a starting point for some of the area's wildest walks, including the tricky Fairfield Horseshoe Walk which takes you up to a summit 2864ft (873 metres) above sea level. For those who like to keep things closer to the ground, this is a great town to wander around. Break off the busy main streets for independent shops and creaky little pubs overlooking the water. There's much to explore in the surrounding area, from impossibly pretty villages to sprawling meadows, deep tarns and endless hiking routes.

# EAT

## THE DRUNKEN DUCK INN AND BARNGATES BREWERY

Ask any food lover where you should eat in the Lake District, and they'll point you to 'The Duck'. This beloved inn sits at a sleepy crossroads a couple of miles outside of Ambleside, with stunning fell views and dairy cows chewing away on the hills. It was once a farmhouse, but has been a pub for 300 years. Its cosy, countryside charm is interspersed with contemporary features – rose-coloured limewash walls, varnished floors, a deep red bar with a garland of dried flowers. As for the food, think elevated pub grub. Every dish is seasonal and lovingly considered, many of them vegan (but you'd never know). The wines are excellent and nicely priced, while all their beer is brewed on-site. *Barngates Brewery* is tucked behind the pub, and all their beers are named after the inn's former pets. Their water comes from nearby Duck Tarn, filtered to perfection to provide the perfect ingredient for their beers. As for the rooms? There are 13 in total, spread across the pub and a dreamy little outhouse across the courtyard.

*Barngates, Ambleside, LA22 0NG*
*drunkenduckinn.co.uk | @drunkenduckinn*

## LAKE ROAD KITCHEN

It can be tricky bagging a table at this multi award-winning restaurant, so book far in advance if you can. There are just a handful of tables in the wood-clad dining room, which is overlooked by the open kitchen headed up by a former Noma chef. It's all about 'hyper-seasonal, climatically local cooking' here, with the option of an eight- or twelve-course menu. The dishes are as beautiful and explosively delicious as you'd expect, showcasing indigenous ingredients, home pickling and resourceful cooking with plenty of Nordic flair. Plus wines from Northern Europe, and an optional extra course dedicated to the best cheeses on the continent. What's one more course, anyway?

*Sussex House, Lake Rd, Ambleside, LA22 0AD*
*lakeroadkitchen.co.uk | @lakeroadkitchen*

## TAP YARD

This welcoming craft beer place serves wood-fired pizzas and charcuterie boards made with good local ingredients – which taste even better after a day walking the surrounding fells. Sitting next to the historic Bridge House in Ambleside's old mill yard, *Tap Yard* has six gleaming copper tanks above the bar, all with brewery-fresh beer (and all Cumbrian, of course).

*Rydal Rd, Ambleside, LA22 9AN | tap-yard.com | @amblesidetapyard*

*he Drunken Duck Inn*

*Above and below: Wabisabi*

## WABISABI

You wouldn't expect to walk through a hidden door into a wood-panelled slice of Japan in Ambleside, but this intrigue is exactly what husband and wife duo Bing and Cara want you to feel. Serving freshly-made sushi and creative bakes throughout the day, it's in the evenings that head chef Bing's 'food dream' comes to life. The nine-course tasting dinner menu takes you through a day in the Lake District. Ours started with an egg dish inspired by dewy mornings, through dishes inspired by misty forests, farms and peaks and ended with a smoky campfire and a vision of the starry, planet-speckled night sky in dessert form. All the produce is sourced locally, or comes from their very own farm. Everything from the hand-sculpted chopstick stands to the ink-splattered dinner plates and block print Japanese tablecloths has been thought through in forensic, heartfelt detail. Bing and Cara are two creatives who want you to love the landscape just as much as they do.

*Compston Rd, Ambleside, LA22 9DJ | wabisabirestaurant.co.uk | @the__wabisabi*

## OLD DUNGEON GHYLL

We're told the *Old Dungeon Ghyll* has been a meeting place for walkers – and their muddy dogs – for over a century. Classic pub food, all home cooked and very satisfying in the face of post-hike hunger, is served in the main Hikers' Bar, which was once the cow stalls (the original exposed beams and stone floors are still intact). Tired adventurers can also find hand-pumped real ale (or whisky, depending on how brutal the journey's been) and 12 bedrooms. There's a great circular walk starting at the pub car park (see page 118).

*Great Langdale, Ambleside, LA22 9JY | odg.co.uk | @olddungeonghyll*

## THE MORTAL MAN

Tucked in the rugged fells of Troutbeck Valley (see page 121), this is the kind of classic Cumbrian pub you'll miss when you go home. In fact, there has been an alehouse on this site since 1689, and famous punters include Coleridge, Hogarth and Wordsworth. Enjoy giant plates of fish and chips, towering burgers made with local produce and free-flowing real ales. The garden is lovely when the sun is shining, with sweeping views of the valley as a backdrop. They also have 12 antiques-filled rooms upstairs, some with four-poster beds.

*Troutbeck, Ambleside, LA23 1PL | themortalman.co.uk*

## STICKLEBARN

A great place to refuel after a day exploring the hills of Great Langdale, this National Trust-run pub celebrates Cumbrian produce with hearty dishes made with Cumbrian meat, bread baked in-house and seasonal produce. There are lots of vegan and vegetarian options on offer, as well as a great wine list and plenty of great whiskies to warm up with. If you want to settle in for a few hours, there's even a film screening room scattered with sofas upstairs.

*B5343, Great Langdale, Ambleside, LA22 9JU*

## CHESTERS BY THE RIVER

On a sunny day, this little slice of land is a bit of a utopia. There are oak trees to snooze under, carpets of wildflowers and lush grass, and the cool, silvery river water. As for Chesters, you'll most likely have to join a queue for the main restaurant. Seats spill out onto a riverside deck, and the food is unusually veg-centric and light. Lunches are seasonal, with offerings like homemade falafel, pea fritters and colourful salad bowls. The on-site bakery is great for takeaways, with salt-speckled chocolate cookies, sourdough sandwiches, sticky cinnamon buns and strong coffees. There's also a shop if you fancy browsing *Nkuku* homeware, linens, candles and locally-made ceramics.

*Skelwith Bridge, Ambleside, LA22 9NJ*
*chestersbytheriver.co.uk | @chestersbytheriver*

*Chesters by the River*

# SLEEP

### BRIMSTONE
This secluded chalet-style hotel has 16 suites, located in the wooded Langdale Estate between Chapel Stile and Elterwater. The whole place has been constructed using natural materials, with a soothing colour palette and plenty of plush corners to unwind – if you can tear yourself away from the fireside in your room. Staff are on hand to give you walking tips, sort out taxi rides or kit you out in free wet-weather gear. And when you're aching after a day on the fells, look no further than the estate's luxurious spa.

*The Langdale Estate, Great Langdale, Ambleside, LA22 9JD*
*brimstonehotel.co.uk | @brimstone.hotel*

### ROTHAY MANOR
This 15-bedroom boutique hotel is a much-loved option for those wishing to stay around Ambleside and Windermere. The design here is classic and luxurious – expect wooden parquet floors, cladded walls painted in serene colours, wallpapered rooms with roll-top baths and fireplaces. The restaurant here has been awarded three AA rosettes for culinary excellence.

*Rothay Bridge, Ambleside, LA22 0EH*
*rothaymanor.co.uk | @rothaymanor*

# EXPLORE

## WALK AND SWIM: STOCK GHYLL FORCE
Stroll behind Lake Road in Ambleside and in less than 10 minutes you'll find Stock Ghyll Force. Keep an eye out for a footpath, which will lead you into beautiful woodland, past tranquil pools and to the famous 70ft (21 metre) waterfall. It's a leisurely circular route (around 2½ miles/3.5km) that will take you around Low Grove, right back into town. Come spring, the trees shade a carpet of daffodils, and the surrounding woodland is brimming with oak trees and indigenous birds. People do swim at the waterfall, and we hear the cold water is lovely on a hot summer's day.

## WALK: OLD DUNGEON GHYLL CIRCULAR
The 7-mile (11-km) Old Dungeon Ghyll Circular is a tough but stunning walk. Beginning at the *Old Dungeon Ghyll* pub (see page 113) car park, you'll climb the toothy edges of Gimmer Crag, returning via the impressive scree runs of Pike o' Stickle. You might have to do a little 'scrambling' (using hands and feet) here, but that can be avoided if you're completely against the idea.

## WALK: THE GREAT AND LITTLE LANGDALE LOOP
The imposing Langdale Pikes (named like creatures in a storybook: Pike o' Stickle, Loft Crag, Harrison Stickle, Pavey Ark, Old Dungeon Ghyll) will be in sight every step of the way on this low-level walk through one of the Lakelands' most scenic valleys. It may be on the easier side, but bear in mind it'll take around 4 hours. Start at Elterwater or Little Langdale, walking along the bottom of Great Langdale until you reach the New (or Old) *Dungeon Ghyll Hotel*. From there, you can head to Blea Tarn for a splash in the silky water. After that, carry on towards Little Langdale and Little Langdale Tarn towards the last leg over Lingmoor Fell. You'll also pass through picture-perfect woodland, postcard villages and crumbling farmhouses along this walk.

## WALK: CATHEDRAL CAVERN
These atmospheric quarries are interlined in a network deep in the woods just above Little Langdale. The main chamber here is what people mean when they refer to the 'Cathedral Cavern'. A great way to get here is by walking, and it'll take you about half an hour from the car park at Tilberthwaite, near Coniston village. Walk towards High Tilberthwaite Farm, following the bridleway on the right-hand side, and across Pierce How Beck you'll spot the Hodge Close spoil heaps. Follow the path to the right after Brooklands Cottage, and you'll find a sign to the tunnels. Be sure to bring a torch for entering the tunnel.

*Starting point: the car park at Tilberthwaite, LA21 8DG*

*Elterwater*

## WALK: TROUTBECK VALLEY

The tranquil Troutbeck Valley lies between Ambleside and Windermere. It's hugged by the slopes of Wansfell and Applethwaite Common, and the Trout Beck river runs all the way down to the shores of Lake Windermere. Popular with walkers in search of ultimate peace, the area is mostly farmland scattered with farmhouses and cottages. The local Jesus Church features windows by the Pre-Raphaelite Sir Edward Burne-Jones. For a scenic circular walk (that'll take you around 2½ hours), start at Brockhole Visitor Centre and follow the track towards Middlerigg Tarn – the route once used by packhorses to carry slate from Troutbeck to the lake. After following Wain Lane, you'll loop back round the Troutbeck Village and end in Brockhole. It's a great way to see the area, and you'll spot some views of Lake Windermere from up high. Drop by *The Mortal Man* for lunch (see page 113) or *The Old Post Office* in the village, where you can fill up on steamy cups of tea, toasted tea cakes and bacon butties.

*Starting point: Brockhole Visitor Centre, LA23 1LJ*

## SHOP: BATH HOUSE

These 'artisans of beauty' have another site in Bowness-on-Windermere, too. The owners are a group of makers from the Lake District, and they sell skincare and fragrances inspired by the beauty of nature. Pop in for scents in artisan glass bottles, hand-poured soaps and natural sponges. The perfect remedy for aching legs.

*The Archway, Market Place, Ambleside, LA22 9BU*
*thebathhouseshop.co.uk | @thebathhouseshop*

## SHOP: KINDRED SPIRITS

Explore a range of small-batch British and locally-crafted spirits in this sunny little shop. They bottle everything for you on the spot, pouring from a wall of giant glass demi-johns. There are also regular tasting evenings, for those who really want to brush up on their whisky knowledge.

*Compston Rd, Ambleside, LA22 9DR | k-spirits.co.uk | @kindredspirits.uk*

### WANDER AND SWIM: ELTERWATER

There are lots of lovely flat walking routes from this gorgeous village, 4 miles (6.5km) west of Ambleside. The most popular is an easy one that takes you along the River Brathay (for as long as you want to keep going), with the Langdale Pikes reflected in the water and plenty of spots for a picnic (or stop for home-spun pizzas, big brunches or a draught ale at *Slates Coffee & Kitchen* on Maple Tree Corner, *slateskitchen.com*). If you're looking for something more challenging, start off at Elterwater car park and follow the Slater's Bridge loop, which will take you past Skelwith Force waterfall, High Park farm and back to Elterwater Bridge. It'll take you around 2 hours to complete. The relatively small lake of Elterwater and its peaceful little bays are just half a mile (0.8km) southeast and we recommend dropping down on its wooded shorelines for an afternoon snooze or swim on a sunny day.

*Starting point: Elterwater car park, LA22 9HP*

### WANDER: LITTLE LANGDALE

On a quiet spring day, this little hamlet is the England of the imagination. Set in the yawning Little Langdale Valley, it's a smattering of blue-tinted stone houses, some with chairs on the porch to look out at the grazing Herdwicks. Sleepy as it is, it's perfect for an afternoon stroll. Ideally ending with a pint at the *Three Shires Inn*, where you'll find great local beers, home-cooked food and an open fire (*threeshiresinn.co.uk*).

### WANDER: CHAPEL STILE VILLAGE

This ridiculously scenic village is 5 miles (8km) north of Ambleside, buried in the mouth of Great Langdale. If you're cycling in the area, this is your stop. The cottages were all built using the blue-ish stone from the surrounding slate quarries, as was the neo-Gothic-style Holy Trinity Church. Pop in for a moment of pure, soul-soothing peace before filling up on old English pub grub at *Wainwright's Inn* (*langdale.co.uk/wainwrights-inn*).

### SWIM: LOUGHRIGG TARN

Loughrigg Tarn is a beautiful small tarn and great sunset swim spot under the skyline of Langdale Pikes. From Ambleside take the A593 towards Coniston and after 1½ miles (2.5km) take a right turn onto a minor road and uphill to a road junction and parking.

*Loughrigg Tarn*

## SWIM: BLEA TARN

We spent a good hour lying on the soft grass here, waiting for the sun to pop out from behind the clouds. When it finally did, we stripped down to our swimsuits and launched ourselves into the water – only realising we weren't alone when we heard a hearty round of applause from a group of elderly women picnicking behind a hill. The water is surprisingly warm (ok, not warm, but not freezing either), and on a clear day the Langdale Pikes are reflected in its still water. From Ambleside, follow the A593 before taking a signposted narrow road to the right for Blea Tarn car park. Follow the path through the pine-scented woods, through an open fell and uphill for sweeping views of the Langdale Valley, and stop at the tarn on your way back.

*Nearest postcode for Blea Tarn car park: LA22 9PG*

## SWIM: GUIDED SWIMMING

If it's your first time swimming in the Lakes, you might want to consider a helping hand from an expert. You'll find these guys in the centre of Ambleside, offering guided wild swims and adventure breaks around the area. They will sort you out with wetsuits and all the open water swimming you'll need to hit the lakes like a local.

*2 Compston St, Ambleside, LA22 9DJ | swimthelakes.co.uk*

## SEE: LOUGHRIGG FELL TRIG POINT

This is one of only a few thousand 'trig points' left in the UK – stone pillars first used in the retriangulation of Great Britain and now treasures of the landscape. They're often made from concrete, but this one is made from local stone. Loughrigg Fell is one of the Lakelands' smaller mountains, peaking at 1099ft (335 metres) above sea level. Following the signs from Rothay Park, you'll reach the summit fairly easily, and be rewarded with 360° views of Grasmere, Windermere and Elterwater.

## SEE: COPT HOWE ROCK CARVINGS

Another mysterious site that's definitely worth a visit if you have an hour or so to spare. These 6000-year-old rock carvings are hidden between Great Langdale Beck and the road to the Pike o' Stickle. Thought to be Neolithic or Bronze Age, there is a collection of abstract shapes, lines and circles carved into this huge boulder. These curious carvings are free to visit and the nearest village is Chapel Stile, a 15-minute drive from Ambleside.

*Blea Tarn*

# CONISTON,
# HAWKSHEAD
# AND NEARBY

# CONISTON, HAWKSHEAD AND NEARBY

Made up of valleys, woodland, vast farmland and pocket-sized villages, the southern lakes are some of the most tranquil in the whole region. You may well be the only swimmer in its whisper-quiet bays, walker in its dream-like forests or the cyclist on its hilly roads. Coniston Water is beloved by wild swimmers and walkers for its peace. This is the place that inspired Arthur Ransome's classic *Swallows and Amazons*. And Beatrix Potter's ivy-clad Hill Top home is close by in Near Sawrey. It's also worth popping into John Ruskin's Brantwood – best approached from the lake by the hourly cruises from Coniston. The famous Old Man of Coniston mountain bears down on its western shore, so the lake is a great place to spend an afternoon on the water.

# EAT

## QUEEN'S HEAD INN

Settle in for an afternoon of ale and comfort food at this 17th-century inn. This place serves great cask ales, and their menu of Cumbrian classics is all made using local, seasonal produce (expect rump of lamb, homemade pies and creamy risottos). Dogs are more than welcome here, and seem to love a snooze by the roaring fire.

*Main Street, Hawkshead, LA22 0NS*
*queensheadhawkshead.co.uk | @queensheadhawkshead*

## STEAM BISTRO

This local restaurant proudly sources their produce from local farmers and producers. The candlelit, brick-lined room is always packed with locals, who feast on fresh fish dishes, Greek-inspired lamb dishes and fresh ravioli. They offer two or three-course set menus and they are not currently licensed, so bring a bottle along with you – they charge a small corkage fee.

*Steam, Tilberthwaite Avenue, Coniston, LA21 8ED*
*steambistro.co.uk | @steambistro*

## THE BLACKSMITHS ARMS

This cosy pub south of Coniston Water in Broughton Mills dates back to 1577, and has been keeping villagers topped up with ale and good food since 1788. Once visited by Coleridge, the pub still has many of its original features, like oak-panelled corridors, large slate floors and heavy oak beams. Sit at the big farmhouse table in the bar to sample some of their local ales, or settle in for a long lunch of locally-sourced comfort classics. This is one of just two Cumbria pubs on CAMRA's national inventory of historic pubs, so it's certainly worth a visit.

*Broughton Mills, Broughton-in-Furness, LA20 6AX*
*theblacksmithsarms.com*

# SLEEP

### THE YEWDALE INN

A perfect base if you want to stay in serene Coniston village. There are nine cosy, well-equipped rooms, some with views over Coniston fell. The pub and restaurant downstairs serve classics made using seasonal, locally-sourced produce (the comfy leather booths are a good spot for a pint of real cask ale, and the fireplace is always burning in the winter). Dogs are welcome inside.

*2 Yewdale Rd, Coniston, LA21 8DU | yewdaleinn.com | @yewdaleinn*

# EXPLORE

### CYCLE AND SWIM: CONISTON WATER

Pick up a mountain, road or e-bike from Lake District Bikes on the southern fringe of Coniston Water to trace the quiet lakeshore to Grizedale Forest (see page 92). This part of the Lakes feels particularly untouristy, and the roads are likely pretty empty as you pass by smoke-coloured old farmhouses and fields full of grazing cattle. Pack a light backpack with a towel and swimwear, and cycle to Low Peel Near at the southern end of Coniston Water. This small bay is usually whisper-quiet, and its shallow shore and still waters are great for less confident swimmers.

*Beck View, Lowick, near Ulverston, LA12 8DX | lakedistrictbikes.com*

### WALK: OLD MAN OF CONISTON

You may have heard of this one. For the ambitious walkers among us, this legendary fell is 2634ft (803 metres) high, and takes around 5 hours to scale. So make sure you're wearing your comfiest walking shoes and prepare for aching legs tomorrow. Head up the east side of the fell from Coniston and circle back behind the fell between Dow Crag, Buck Pike and Brown Pike. Another option is to go via the mountain tarn of Goat's Water. It's a longer route, but you'll pass fewer tourists on your way. However you reach the top, the views are unsurprisingly jaw-dropping. For detailed route guidance and information about elevation, check out: *thinkadventure.co.uk*.

### WALK: COPPERMINES VALLEY WALK

Begin this walk at the *Black Bull* (*blackbullconiston.co.uk*), taking the track out of Coniston along the edge of Church Beck. After that, you'll pass over Miner's Bridge into the lush and scarred valley, which lies above Coniston. Walk along the path toward Levers Water dam, where you'll be able to take in Boulder Valley's rock formations – including the wonderfully-named Pudding Stone boulder. The circular walk (which is pleasant and doesn't require much climbing) will take you about 2½ hours. There are quite a few disused mine entrances, so keep dogs on leads and an eye on children.

*Starting point: Black Bull Inn and Hotel, LA21 8DU*

Coniston Water

## WALK: TARN HOWS

Overlooked by the Coniston hills and Langdale Pikes, the enormous Tarn Hows is a classic dog-walking spot and is fully accessible for wheelchair users on the whole path around. The less than 2-mile (3-km) walk around the Tarn will take you about 30–40 minutes, so it is a good option to fit in before breakfast or in between rainstorms. There is quick access to the water's edge from the car park 2 miles (3km) north of Coniston (use the postcode LA22 0PP). We recommend the tree-lined arm of land that juts into the water for prime picnicking.

## SEE: TOM GILL WATERFALL

If you're exploring Coniston, don't miss this fast-flowing staircase of waterfalls. Start at the Tarn Hows National Trust car park. You'll see a sign for Tom Gill as you follow the path down to the water, through the gate. Carry on up the hill after you reach the first waterfall to the second, which stands tall and reflects the surrounding trees and flowers on a clear day.

*Starting point: Tarn Hows National Trust car park, LA21 8DP*

## PADDLEBOARD: CONISTON WATER

While we struggle to stay upright for more than a few seconds at a time, we both agree that paddleboarding is one of the best ways to get out on the water and take in the surroundings – especially on a sunny day. Unlike the larger lakes in the area, Coniston Water is almost always calm, making it perfect for a sport that requires a lot of balance. You can rent a board for up to 2 hours, and the friendly team will talk you through all the techniques to stay upright on the water. Or you could do what we do and sit on the board, taking in the Old Man of Coniston in the background. Check Coniston Boating Centre's website for safety tips, and make sure you call ahead to check if the weather conditions are good for your trip.

*Coniston Boating Centre, Lake Rd, Coniston, LA21 8AN*
*conistonboatingcentre.co.uk*

*Tarn Hows*

CARTMEL
AND NEARBY

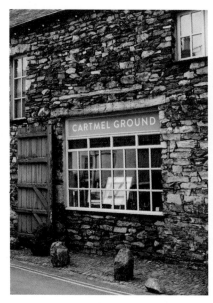 

# CARTMEL AND NEARBY

Cartmel is now the first image that comes into my mind when we think of the villages of the Lake District. We think of it as sweet and delicious, but that may just be down to it being the home of sticky toffee pudding (both our favourites, in case you were wondering). This perfect little village is on the southern edge of the Lake District, not far from the River Eea. It's flanked by fields and farmland, with an ancient square and 12th-century priory. It's definitely worth staying here for a night or two, not least because it has some of the best pubs and restaurants in the whole area. We had a glorious evening wandering past tiny alleys and trickling streams, ending with a feast at the pub and a chat with a local painter over our second bowl of sticky toffee. A night well spent, we think.

# EAT

## CARTMEL COFFEE

Pop into this pistachio-green coffee shop for breakfasts of toasted tea cakes or crumpets, or come for hearty, classic lunches of potted shrimp, chunky Cheddar sandwiches or the obligatory bacon sandwich on granary.

*The Well House, The Square, Cartmel, LA11 6QB | @cartmel.coffee*

## THE CAVENDISH ARMS HOTEL AND RESTAURANT

Cartmel locals crowd this homely pub in the centre of town. The 450-year-old coaching inn has low-beamed ceilings, thick stone walls and an open fire, making it the perfect place to while away a few hours with local beer and English comfort food made with the best local produce. It's also a hotel, with a handful of comfy and classic rooms overlooking the river.

*Cavendish Street, Cartmel, LA11 6QA*
*thecavendisharms.co.uk | @cavendisharmscartmel*

## THE MALLARD

Let's face it, tea rooms are crucial on any Lake District trip. This one is primed for hungry walkers in search of giant Cumberland sausage buns, bacon toasties and scoops of double Jersey ice cream.

*Devonshire Buildings, Cartmel, LA11 6PN*
*unsworthsyard.co.uk/mallard-tea-shopnest | @themallardteashop*

## L'ENCLUME

Simon Rogan's celebrated Cartmel restaurant holds two Michelin stars and was named the UK's number one restaurant by The Good Food Guide in 2020. It's no surprise, then, that the food is mindblowing. Produce comes from their very own farm, so the ingredients are always hyper-seasonal and local. In fact, you can pay the farm a visit and see the edible flowers, towering vegetable patches and juicy fruit trees for yourself. The menu changes constantly, and every dish is creative, thoughtful and full of pride. As will you be after bagging a table here. If you're looking for a place to stay in Cartmel, L'Enclume has 16 plush rooms for guests to stay in. Like the restaurant, they fill up way ahead of time, so be sure to secure a booking in advance.

*Cavendish Street, Cartmel, LA11 6QA | lenclume.co.uk*

On the chalkboard:

Sweets

Chocolate cremeux Hazelnut & tonka bean ice

Homemade sticky toffee pudding vanilla ice cream

Lemon curd pavlova, raspberry, pistac

Greek yoghurt & honey mousse granola, candied

3 Scoops Lakeland ice cream

Cheese board selection

**Above:** *The Cavendish Arms Hotel and Restaurant*
**Below:** *L'Enclume*

# EXPLORE

## SHOP: CARTMEL VILLAGE SHOP

The actual home of sticky toffee pudding. They started making it over 20 years ago, and the rest is British pudding history. Stock up on their original-recipe pudding, which is as treacly, gooey and glossy as you'd expect, and throw in a few chocolate and lemon variations while you're there. You can also find fresh farm produce and artisanal preserves.

*Parkgate House, 1 The Square, Cartmel, LA11 6QB*
*cartmelvillageshop.co.uk*

## SHOP: UNSWORTH'S YARD

Overlooked by a 12th-century priory, this little patchwork of producers and shops is a great place to spend the evening. You'll find Unsworth's Yard's very own brewery in the courtyard, with the door always open for tours, tastings and chats. For frosty glasses of white or rich red wines, head next door to Cartmel Drinkshop. It's also home to Cartmel Cheeses, where wheels of local cheeses are piled high behind a glass door.

*Unsworth's Yard, Ford Rd, Cartmel, Cumbria, LA11 6PN | unsworthsyard.co.uk*

## SHOP: PERFECT ENGLISH

Treat yourself to beautiful homewares from this mother-and-daughter-run shop in Cartmel Square. They have a small collection of hand-picked furniture pieces, handmade skincare, textiles, candles and pretty much everything else you could need to turn your house into the perfect contemporary Lake District haven.

*7 The Square, Cartmel, LA11 6QB | perfectenglishshop.co.uk*

## SEE: CARTMEL PRIORY

If you're staying in Cartmel Village on a weekend, you'll wake to the sound of the priory's bells summoning worshippers to service every Sunday morning. Head to the ancient chapel to see intricate carvings, stained glass windows and beautiful Renaissance screens.

*The Priory Church of St Mary and St Michael, Cartmel, LA11 6QD*
*cartmelpriory.org.uk*

## WANDER: EGGERSLACK AND HAMPSFIELD WOOD

This summit of this ancient woodland gives way to stunning views across Morecambe Bay and the Lake District Mountain. It is bursting with native trees, ferns and flowers – especially in the spring when you'll find thousands of bluebells carpeting the floor. It has plenty of footpaths, so you can make your walk as short or long as you like.

*Nearest postcode for parking along Hampsfell Rd: LA11 6BD*

# ULLSWATER

# ULLSWATER

The very place that inspired Wordsworth to pen his most famous poem, 'I Wandered Lonely as a Cloud'. Glimmering from the eastern fringes of the national park, this is the second biggest lake in the District – a mere 7½ miles (12km) long, to be exact, with some of the region's most staggering fells lining it. Patterdale can be found at the southern end and Pooley Bridge to the north, while Penrith is the nearest market town. Northeast of Ullswater, towards Penrith, is the charming village of Askham. The Ullswater Way is a 20-mile (32-km) walking route that traces the entire lake; you can do the whole thing in a day, or hop aboard one of the local 'steamers' to break it up a little. But if you're having trouble deciding where to get off, remember that Alfred Wainwright called the sloping, dry stone wall-lined walk from Glenridding to Howtown 'the most beautiful of lake walks in the National Park'. So that's a good place to start.

*The Queen's Head*

# EAT

### LOWTHER BARN TEA ROOM
There are plenty of places to fill up on sugary goodness around Ullswater. This old stone barn is in a particularly lovely setting, on the Glenridding and Howtown stretch of the Ullswater Way, with a scattering of outdoor tables overlooking the water. It is only accessible by foot or bike.

*Beckside Farm, Sandwick Martindale, Penrith, CA10 2NF | becksidefarm.com*

### THE QUEEN'S HEAD
This 17th-century pub in the heart of Askham describes their ever-changing menu as 'super-posh pub food'. Everything is made using hyper-local produce grown and reared on their farms (they're part of the Askham Collection, which includes *Askham Hall* and the *George and Dragon*, see page 82). Expect game, fresh fish, puddings made with fruit from the Askham Kitchen Garden's trees and local Cumbrian ales. Come Sundays, they do a three-course lunch. Booking is a must, as there are just nine tables in the restaurant. And if you want to stay, they have six cosy, plush bedrooms for a pretty reasonable nightly rate.

*Askham, Penrith, CA10 2PF | queensheadaskham.co.uk | @queensheadaskham*

### THE KITCHEN GARDEN CAFÉ
The gardens at Askham Hall are bursting with vegetables, pigs rolling in the mud, damson trees, grazing sheep and hotbeds of beetroot and rhubarb. Come to the Kitchen Garden Café on a Friday evening in summer and you'll smell pizzas cooking in the wood-fired oven. You can't pre-book a table, so just head there early to bed down at a table overlooking the River Lowther.

*Askham Hall, Askham, Penrith, CA10 2PF | askhamhall.co.uk | @askham_hall*

# SLEEP

### ANOTHER PLACE

Found down a gravely tree-lined path, this laid-back (but luxurious) hotel lies on the shores of Ullswater, and is a home-away-from-home for stylish city dwellers and visitors in search of utter peace. Its famous swimming pool has a floor-to-ceiling glass wall for views of the fells and lake during your laps. In the spa, you can unwind with 'freestyle massages', body scrubs and manicures. The interior is all wood-panelled walls in shades of emerald, olive and grey, seagrass carpets and velvet sofas. There's an opulent living room (for adults only in the evening) where you can play board games and sip G&Ts by the open fire. Outside, wooden deck chairs face the mountains and water, with a few orange hammocks strung up on the ancient oak trees. In the lobby, you'll find the week's activities chalked up on a board, from stand-up paddleboarding to morning lake swims – all setting off from the private jetty. Downstairs, there's a casual restaurant for lunch and dinner, but you'll want to book a table at the more formal Rampsbeck (where, if you're lucky, you'll be eating with a view of the moon lighting up the lake).

*Rampsbeck Grange, Watermillock, Ullswater, CA10 2LP*
*another.place | @anotherplacehotels*

*Another Place*

*Askham Kitchen Garden Café*

# EXPLORE

## WALK: HALLIN FELL
This fell is a mere 1273ft (388 metres) high, so it's perfect for a little afternoon walk when you're not quite in the mood for Scafell Pike. Hop on an Ullswater Steamer to Howtown and follow signs for Martindale Church. You'll reach the summit in around 45 minutes, and at the top you'll find incredible views of Ullswater and beyond.

*Starting point: Pooley Bridge Pier, CA10 2NN; Glenridding Pier, CA11 0US*

## WALK: HIGH STREET SUMMIT AND SMALL WATER TARN
Named after the Roman road that crosses its plateau, High Street is a wide, grassy summit in the far eastern region of the national park. At its peak, you'll find expansive views of the Eastern Fells. It's far less trodden than some of the more popular peaks in the area, so you might even find yourself taking in the views alone. Starting from Cow Bridge car park (near Hartsop on the southern tip of Ullswater), walk via Hayeswater Gill and head directly up via The Knott. It'll take you around 2½ hours.

*Starting point: Cow Bridge car park, CA11 0NZ*

## WALK AND SWIM: ANGLE TARN
Beginning at the car park in Patterdale, walk on the Stony Rigg before reaching Angletarn Pikes. From here, you can see Angle Tarn for the first time, invitingly blue and peppered with little grassy islands. The hard-going walk is worth it, as there are views across Ullswater from up here, and you'll get an eyeful of the Far Eastern Fells too. Descend to Angle Tarn, where the water is surprisingly cool and comfortable for a swim, with perfect banks for reading or snoozing in the sun. The banks are also a favourite for campers, who spend starry nights sheltered in the small valley and wake up to 360° views of the mountains (although remember you need permission from the land owner). If you don't feel like swimming, a loop of the tarn is lovely in itself and is around 5 miles (8km) in total.

*Starting point: Patterdale car park, CA11 0NN*

## WANDER: ASKHAM
Take a little time to wander this charming little village, where cottages are perched on sloping hills with pear trees climbing up their walls. It adjoins the River Lowther, and the upper section of the village has beautiful views of Lowther Castle and the sweeping landscape beyond. Picturesque, peaceful and full of Cumbrian stone-built cottages. You may have heard of *Askham Hall*, home to a Michelin-starred restaurant, which is definitely worth a splurge. When the gardens are open, you can also stop by at the *Kitchen Garden Café* (see page 149).

*askhamhall.co.uk | @askham_hall*

## CANOE: ULLSWATER CANOE TRAIL

Rent a canoe from Glenridding Sailing Centre to set off for a day on
Ullswater (*glenriddingsailingcentre.co.uk*). There are a couple of beautiful
trails recommended. The first starts at the Dunmallard car park in Pooley
Bridge, paddling southwest past Gale Bay, Waterside, Ullswater Yacht
Club, Sharrow Bay and Howtown Wyke, where you can stop for lunch.
Another launches from Glenridding, where you can shore up in Aira
Green for afternoon tea. Alternatively, you can just do a circular paddle
of the lake – for as long as you feel you manage. It's the perfect way to
take in the clear water, shadowy fells and colourful foliage on the shores.

*Do be sure always to wear a lifejacket out on the water, even if you're
experienced. The weather can change fast and winds can pick up unexpectedly.
Always try to canoe in a small group, and wear plenty of layers to stay warm.*

*Glenridding Sailing Centre, The Spit, CA11 0PE | edenriverstrust.org.uk*

## SWIM: KAILPOT CRAG

Considered by many to be the best spot in the Lake District for a dip,
you'll most likely find yourself completely alone here. To arrive at the
rugged open crag, board the ferry to Howtown pier and walk southwest
along the lake path. After passing lots of sparling bays and pine woods,
you'll find Kailpot Crag – recognisable for its ancient vegetation and little
shingle beach. You can dive in from a small cliff, and the deep waters are
perfect for taking in the early morning light or evening sun.

## SWIM: GLENCOYNE BAY

This tranquil pebbled beach is a popular spot for canoers to launch into
Ullswater, and you can easily park in the car park opposite the shore.
The relatively shallow water's edge and calm waters make this bay the
perfect place for less confident swimmers – who may just want to wade
in the shallows and watch the swans floating on the surface. As well as
being a great launching spot for a day's adventures on the water, the bay
has spectacular views of the craggy peaks and surrounding hill farms.

*Nearest postcode for parking: CA11 0NQ*

## SEE: AIRA FORCE WATERFALL

Park in the Aira Force car park, about 5 miles (8km) west of Ullswater.
Set off up the path into the woodland. There's a gentle ascent before
you reach the path that dips down and around the famous Aira Force
waterfall. Take a flask of coffee and perch on one of the rocks looking
down at the water, folded into the fern-covered hills and ancient trees.

*Penrith, CA11 0JS*

*Left to right:* Aira Force walk, Ullswater

## CYCLE: LOWTHER CASTLE AND GARDENS

There's a beautiful network of cycling trails in the Lowther Estate (about 20 minutes in the car from Ullswater) which is made up of 19th-century castle ruins and manicured gardens. Cycling is easy on these quiet paths, with very little traffic and some of the most beautiful views in the area. The estate is now working with Arragons Cycles, so you can hire classic push bikes or electric ones if you're feeling lazy (which we were).

*Lowther Castle, CA10 2HH | lowthercastle.org*

## RIDE: PARK FOOT PONY TREKKING

One of the most beautiful ways to take in the dramatic surrounds of Ullswater is on horseback. Park Foot Trekking is run by Claire Cowx, who has a paddock full of family-friendly ponies. There are around five outings a day, ranging from half an hour to an hour. The fell treks take you uphill from the stables, through brooks and heathery hills, with dramatic views of Ullswater lake below. Don't expect a high octane journey – the rocky terrain means the horses stick to a leisurely stroll. All the better for taking in the scenery, we reckon.

*Howtown Rd, Pooley Bridge, CA10 2NA*
*ponytrekkingullswater.co.uk*

## SAIL: ST PATRICK'S BOAT LANDING

Ullswater just so happens to be our favourite lake. It's huge, with the most mighty surroundings, and looks beautiful at just about any time of year. Rent a boat and spend a few hours on the water with St Patrick's self-drive motor boats, rowing boats or canoes. We recommend bringing a jumper, towel and a flask of something hot if you plan to dive in. Which you should, of course. Open seasonally, check website for details. As with all boating expeditions, be sure to follow the guidelines and wear a life jacket.

*St Patrick's Boat Landing, Glenridding, CA11 0QQ*
*stpatricksboatlanding.co.uk*

*Park Foot Pony Trekking*

# INDEX